WOMEN
of a
GENEROUS
SPIRIT

TOUCHING OTHERS WITH
LIFE-GIVING LOVE

WOMEN
of a
GENEROUS
SPIRIT

LOIS MOWDAY RABEY

WATERBROOK
PRESS

COLORADO SPRINGS

WOMEN OF A GENEROUS SPIRIT
PUBLISHED BY WATERBROOK PRESS
5446 North Academy Boulevard, Suite 200
Colorado Springs, Colorado 80918
A division of Bantam Doubleday Dell Publishing Group, Inc.

Scriptures in this book, unless otherwise noted, are from
The Holy Bible: New International Version, copyright 1973, 1978, 1984,
International Bible Society, Zondervan Bible Publishers.
Any italics in Scripture quotes are the author's.

ISBN 1-57856-050-0

Copyright © 1998 by Lois Mowday Rabey
Published in association with the literary agency of
Alive Communications, Inc., 1465 Kelly Johnson Blvd.
Suite 320, Colorado Springs, CO 80920

Printed in the United States of America

1998—First Edition
10 9 8 7 6 5 4 3 2 1

FOR ELIZABETH D. CORNWELL,

my mother and a woman of a generous spirit

Contents

Acknowledgments

There are always many people to thank after the process of writing a book comes to a close. At the risk of neglecting someone, I want to thank some of the people who have touched my life in generous ways, giving me encouragement and hope:

Kathy Yanni, my agent and friend. Thank you, Kathy, for all the words, notes, phone calls, and expressions of care that communicate your belief in me. I am greatly appreciative for all your professional help and especially for the opportunity to be part of a friendship that has enriched my life.

Liz Heaney, my editor and friend. Our conversations began over lasagna and maps of Italy and have progressed to the nitty-gritty stuff of the details of writing. I am so grateful for your expertise and insight. Thank you for helping craft this book into the finished product. You're a wonderful editor and a new friend that I look forward to knowing better.

Dan Rich, Scharlotte Rich, Rebecca Price, and the staff at WaterBrook. This publishing experience has been a deeply fulfilling and pleasant process for me. Thank you all for making me feel so welcome and for your continuing encouragement.

Lara Van Hulzen and April Young, wonderful interviewers who assisted me in gathering some of the stories in this book.

The many women who gave of their time to allow me to interview them.

Traci Mullins, Judy Couchman, and Jerry Jones, my friends who are part of the writing community of Colorado Springs. Thank you all for so many hours of asking questions and listening to my ramblings and still being willing to talk again. Your words have meant a great deal to me, and I value your friendships greatly. And thanks, Traci, for "talking me down from the ledge."

Lu Dunbar, Libby Paddle, and Lara Van Hulzen, who read the unedited manuscript and provided helpful insight and suggestions.

And finally, thank you to my family—Steve; Chadd, Lisa, Justin, and Alex Miller; Craig, Lara, and Lisa Van Hulzen. You all bless my life in ways too numerous to count every single day.

Chapter 1

Life-Giving Women

Life-giving women.

We all know some . . . women we call when we need to talk, women we gravitate toward for encouragement and hope, friends we know will be excited to hear our good news. Women who graciously accept our interruptions and touch us with their love. They give of themselves, their time, and their possessions.

Women of a generous spirit.

They greet everyone they meet with a breath of life: a smile, an acknowledgment, a kind word that reflects genuine caring beneath the simple courtesy. They touch with love: sometimes with the deep significance of friendship and sometimes with the light touch of a caring stranger.

We are drawn to them when we walk into a room full of strangers. Their approachable demeanor and warm greetings assure us of acceptance. They make eye contact and smile at us as we search the room for a safe place to linger.

Such women are life-givers.

I know this firsthand.

THEY INVITE US IN

Every year I make at least one trip back to Ft. Lauderdale, Florida. I lived there for fourteen years and grew to love the ocean, fabulous seafood, and tropical ambiance, but those enticements are not what continue to draw me away from my home in Colorado. It isn't even the warm weather since I enjoy the brisk chill of western winters. I go to spend time with my friend Claudette. Our days are filled with the usual female stuff—shopping, lunch, talking, dinner, talking, talking, and more talking. But the highlight of my trip is the time we spend each morning at her kitchen table.

After her husband leaves for work and before the phone starts to ring, we sit with our coffee and talk. Her worn, thick Bible resides on one side of the table with a notepad and pen on top of it. Claudette's red-framed, granny glasses are nearby, and her cockatiel, Blancita, sits on her shoulder. The sun streams through the window and splashes across the table as the shadows of palm branches dance in the light.

Claudette's life and mine have many parallels. We were both widowed, have grown children and grandchildren, and have both remarried. We became friends shortly after my first husband, Jack, was killed in a hot-air balloon accident. I was thirty-four years old. But God poured his indefinable love into the chasms of pain in my soul and rescued me from personal despair. Claudette's generous spirit was one of the ways he accomplished that healing.

The first time I sat at her kitchen table was just months after Jack's death. Claudette had called to invite me to come over and talk, and though we hadn't met, her reputation had preceded her, and I eagerly accepted her offer. I drank deeply of the hope she poured into the hurting places of my life. Claudette asked questions about how I felt. Her eyes held my gaze without the shifting discomfort I had come to expect when I talked about the gnawing ache of loneliness. She didn't fill the silence with words or verses of Scripture. Often she just sat with me and let me ramble as I tried to integrate the reality of my faith with my broken heart. When she did speak, she didn't offer solutions. Her words were few: a touch on my wringing hands and a soft "I know." Her compassionate eyes said the rest. She absorbed some of my pain and hurt with me.

Claudette gave me hope. She had suffered a similar loss, yet the optimism she showed withstood scrutiny. It was no sugarcoated religious cliché that she pulled out of some spiritual name-it-and-claim-it box. She told me the truth. The fullness of her life was entwined with threads of grief. Claudette's life showed me that peace and pain can coexist.

Through her, I came to believe that I *could* experience joy again.

My daughters and I began to laugh and look forward to days that weren't consumed with piercing pain. Over the course of many months, Claudette gently and continually brought me back to the truth of God's love. She didn't preach; she just softly reminded me that God loved me and would heal me.

Eighteen years later I'm still receiving from Claudette. She's a life-giver. Though thousands of miles apart, we talk across the miles several times a week, and she still supplies large doses of love and truth. She knows my heart and carefully handles my joys and hurts. She's available, interested, thoughtful, and firmly anchored in her faith. After being with her, in person or over the phone lines, I am lifted, energized, encouraged.

I'm so glad I responded to Claudette's invitation to come over and talk; we have developed a deep and time-weathered friendship. But some women need more than an invitation to talk; they need others to draw them out, and that's what life-giving women do.

THEY DRAW OTHERS OUT

Women of a generous spirit offer a loving touch or a kind word to a friend who has withdrawn or to a person they have just met. They live out the truth of these words: "Pleasant words are a honeycomb, sweet to the soul and healing to the bones" (Proverbs 16:24).

One such generous spirit crossed my path and touched me when I didn't even know I was hurting.

"Excuse me," she said. "Is it okay for me to be in here?"

I hadn't noticed her approaching me. I must have momentarily closed my eyes. I was so tired. It had been so pleasant; the lone musician playing and singing his hauntingly beautiful songs in the peaceful emptiness of the church. The preconcert sound check had become a private performance for me. Now my tranquillity was disturbed.

"I don't know," I replied, trying not to sound annoyed.

"I'm here with my husband who is back in the narthex, meeting with some people. I just came up here near the front and sat down."

I smiled faintly and avoided direct eye contact.

She sat down. I was on the end of a row of pews, and she sat down in front of me. She swung around and rested her arms on the back of the pew. I knew my reverie was over—I had to look up and talk to this woman. I had to be sociable.

"Why are you here so early?" she asked.

"We know John Michael," I explained. As I looked into the eyes of this would-be intruder, my annoyance dissipated. Something in her smile disarmed my defenses. I continued, "My husband, Steve, and John Michael have written a book together, and we came up here for Steve to meet with him before the concert."

For the next hour, Corky and I talked like old friends. I heard about her kids and her beautician business, her work at the hospital, and her love for Jesus. I told her about my writing and speaking, my grandson, and our next grandbaby due in six months. We both teared up as she told me of two miscarriages she had had, and I told her of my older daughter having had a miscarriage the previous summer.

As the doors of the church opened, people streamed in, and our conversation blended in with others. Corky introduced me to her friends, and I introduced her to Steve. We exchanged phone numbers, and I arranged to interview her for this book.

Our encounter would not seem extraordinary to an onlooker. We were two women striking up a conversation and carrying it on for an hour. Happens all the time. Women talk to each other. But, for me, that was no routine meeting. I had entered it reluctantly, begrudgingly. I was tired and had wanted to sit quietly alone. But by the time the conversation ended, I felt energized and encouraged.

On the way home, Steve asked me about it.

"She touched me," I told him. "I think she was an angel."

This stranger listened to me and heard me. She sat down in front of me full of love, and she gave some of it away. She came like a gardener watering thirsty plants that happened to be in her path, and there I was. I hadn't even known I was thirsty.

Steve and I had been away from home for several months, and it had been a long time since I had sat and talked with another woman about my family and my work. Corky temporarily filled the gap that my friends usually filled. We shared the easy conversation of giving and receiving that women bring to one another. It was a refreshing moment in the middle of a busy, but lonely, time. I felt better for having met her.

THEY GIVE FROM AN UNSEEN REALITY

Women of a generous spirit have another distinctive characteristic: They give from an unseen reality. Life-giving women fill up and give out in ways that nourish themselves and give life to others. They know God, believe him, and live a faith-filled life. They seem to have something more—more than just head knowledge or blind obedience. They experience a relationship with God that transcends their circumstances. Somewhere deep inside their souls, they commune with him in ways that transform their minds and lives. That is why Claudette was able to walk with me in my pain—and why she is able to give to others in the midst of her own.

The phone rang early one July morning, and Claudette's broken voice whispered across the miles.

"What's wrong?" I asked.

"Brian's gone."

Claudette's grandson had finally been released from his struggle with a rare birth disorder that had caused him to deteriorate over the years. We'd had many somber conversations about Claudette's daughter, Cissie, and her agony at watching one of her children slip away from her.

"How are you?" I asked.

"This one is heavy."

My tears hit the mouthpiece of the phone and slithered down around the twisted cord. I bit my lip to keep from sobbing aloud. I didn't speak.

"I'll call you later when I get back from Cissie's," Claudette said.

"Okay."

I hung up the phone and cried on and off for several days. I didn't have any grandchildren myself then, but my friend's pain pierced my heart.

She called when she got back to Florida from the funeral. Her voice sounded so weak, and I could picture her in bed with the blinds shut.

"I'm tuckin' in for a while," she explained.

"I know."

I did know. For years I had watched Claudette walk in confidence with her Lord. She "tucks in" when she needs God's healing. I knew what her routine would be. She would rest for the balance of the day. Then she and Carlos would go out for something to eat, and that evening she would call Cissie and encourage her. During the night, she would dwell on verses of Scripture to ease the fears that darkness brings. In the morning, she would sit at the kitchen table with her Bible open. She would weep her grief out to him over the next few days and continue to affirm her belief in his love and care.

The actions themselves would not bring her relief. They were simply reflections of Claudette's response to the hidden, mysterious breath of God sustaining her spirit. Her actions were the visible confirmation that she had been living elsewhere—a private place where her Father could heal her soul.

Several days later I picked up the phone. "Hi, sweetie." The southern drawl was stronger than before.

"Hi," I said.

"Well, I'm peekin' my head out a little. It's gonna take awhile to make it through a day without crying, but I'm filled with his peace."

She sounded sad but assured. We spoke of heaven and Brian's meeting with the grandfather he had never known. I pictured my Jack nearby and let my tears flow freely. After a few minutes, Claudette asked how I was doing.

She was back to giving. She had drawn deeply from the bottomless reserves of God's love and, in the unseen places of her heart, had vulnerably laid herself open to the healing mystery of his touch. She had placed her empty, hurting soul at his feet and believed in the work he would do to restore her. And when she was filled again with his strength, she had come back.

Women of a generous spirit, like Corky and Claudette, come to every circumstance and relationship full. The edges around their personalities are smooth. They are not easily jarred or offended by intrusions and interruptions. They experience a strange inner calm that permeates even deep pain. They notice others. They touch warmly and ask sincerely. And when they are living in seasons of receiving, they receive graciously.

They are honest when they are unable to express their generosity. If something in their lives is out of balance, they don't blame or complain or make excuses. They tell the truth. And they retreat to the source of their strength. The result? God fills them with life-giving love that impacts others and enriches their own lives.

BECOMING LIFE-GIVERS

If you are like me and most women I meet, you are probably saying to yourself, *I would love to be that kind of woman, but I think it's an impossible ideal for me. I want to be life-giving, but I can hardly keep up with my life. I read Proverbs 31 and feel guilty—that woman gives endlessly and doesn't even seem to need sleep! I just don't have that kind of energy. I already feel overwhelmed; I'm so busy. How can I do anything more?*

Believe me, I know how you feel. Part of my decision to write this book grew from the realization that I had all but given up my own attempts to be a generously giving woman. I had tried to be like them and had failed. The ideal seemed too difficult to achieve.

My typical response to any problem has been: "Just tell me what to do!" If I am in a difficult circumstance, feel badly, want change, I step up to the bar, pound my fist on the counter, and demand the recipe for success. I have been deluded by the philosophy in the popular advertisement for athletic shoes, JUST DO IT!

When I first realized that I wanted to be a woman of a generous spirit, I thought I simply had to copy a set of behaviors. I decided to act warm, gentle, kind, caring. Trouble is, my behavior change never lasted. Soon I found myself reverting back to my old self-centered ways. Next I tried turning up the heat on my religious practices. I read the Bible more, prayed more specifically, and went to church every week. Something was still wrong. My cookie-cutter approach wasn't working. When circumstances came into my life that depleted me and left me empty, I convinced myself that generous women can give to others because their lives are pain-free.

But that's a lie. They suffer just like the rest of us—the difference is that they have a power that allows them to get through difficulties and be life-givers again.

The stories in this book are about women like you and me, women who get tired and discouraged and struggle with the pains of life. But they are also women who are becoming women of a generous spirit. Their experiences and wisdom can encourage each of us to keep trying. We can lay down our images of perfection and begin to explore how we can touch others. Each of us can become a life-giving woman. It is an adventure in God-discovery that can change us and free us. As we grow more like him, we are released from the bondage of trying to copy some unreachable ideal.

WE ARE THE IDEAL

The good news is that the ideal I long for is inside of me, and the ideal you long for is inside of you. But we do not become those ideals by becoming clones of the women who already live as generous spirits. We can learn from them and be encouraged by them, but we don't become *them*. We become who God intends each of us to be.

We change from the inside out. What we see in these women is the external evidence of internal realities. We see the fruit of their continuing inner growth in relationship with God.

Being a woman of a generous spirit is not a destination to aim for. It is the by-product of a relationship, a process, in which we get to know God. Life-giving love spills out of us as a result. God changes us from within. That is worth pursuing.

Before we look at the gifts that generous women give, we need to consider some of our perspectives. Let's look beneath the surface of our own lives in order to avoid merely changing our behavior. We need to allow God to change our hearts . . . to change us from within.

Questions and Suggestions

Many of these suggestions require writing down your thoughts. So, get a notebook, journal, or file on your computer, and begin to record your adventure. Be brutally honest. This is for you and God alone.

1. Write a paragraph describing the woman you would like to become.

2. Now write a paragraph that describes how you see yourself today.

3. List some women who have touched you in life-giving ways. How?

4. Describe ways that you are inviting to others. Describe ways that you are not inviting.

5. Describe ways that you seek others out. Describe ways you do not seek others out.

6. Don't worry about making changes yet.

Section One

✿

GAINING
PERSPECTIVE

Chapter 2

What Are My True Motives?

I was fourteen when I first realized God's love for me. My girlfriend invited me to a Bible camp for a week in August. I went with no spiritual expectations whatsoever. If someone had asked me, I would have said that my life was just fine. I liked school, had lots of good friends, and couldn't wait for the kickoff of the football season, marking another year of cheering our state-ranked athletic teams to headline coverage.

The first few days of camp were filled with predictable summer fun. We hiked to the lake and swam and paddled canoes and drenched ourselves in baby oil to speed up the sun's last chance to bronze our bodies. My friend and I speculated about whether girls as young as we were could ever snag an appreciative glance or compliment from one of our adorable, college-age camp counselors.

Tuesday night was clear and brisk. We huddled around a blazing campfire that slightly stung our sunburned faces. I remember sitting with my knees tucked up under my oversized sweatshirt, basking in the security of friendship and fun. Several counselors started strumming guitars, and the resident pastor for that week opened our campfire time with a prayer. He held an open Bible as he began to talk about Jesus.

I had attended church on and off all my life, but my attendance was perfunctory, the thing most people did. My parents were not religious, and we never talked about God being relevant to our lives. In fact, the only time my father said anything about God was in anger.

As the pastor talked, a chill penetrated my feelings of security. He was talking about God loving and accepting us completely. He said that God's love was unconditional. His words touched a pain I had managed to keep buried beneath layers of denial. My father loved me, and I knew it. Sure, he got angry—but didn't everyone? Sure, he yelled and said hurtful things and then withdrew into stony silence. Didn't a lot of fathers? In the middle of the yelling and the silence, I had learned to choreograph a dance designed to win back his love. Sometimes I stumbled into the right steps, and my father's love was once again bestowed. Other times, my dance brought no applause, and I just kept trying.

That night in August of 1959 I cried at the thought of receiving God's unconditional love. The ice in my soul began to melt. I heard about Jesus. He was inviting me to live with him, and he would live in me. He would come into my heart and change my life. I bowed my head and closed my eyes and prayed. The strains of the chorus "Kum-Ba-Ya" were drifting around our circle as many of us began our lives in Christ.

I determined to serve and follow Jesus always. My heart was full of love and gratitude for the immeasurable gift of his sacrificed life on the cross in my place. I wanted to be a generous young woman.

The years passed, and giving didn't come as easily as it had at first. I still loved Jesus and longed to be the woman he wanted me to be, but I didn't feel the power or the fullness that had so ignited me in those early days. Looking back, I see that other motivations had quietly replaced my original motivation of gratitude, hindering my ability to be truly life-giving.

A SUBTLE SHIFT

Our motivations are those thoughts, impressions, emotions, and beliefs that propel us into action. Many times they are unconscious influences that whisper which way we should go and what we should do.

When we first encounter Jesus, our hearts overflow with gratitude. We savor his forgiveness and acceptance. Aware of the fullness of his love, we give to give God pleasure. We want to please him. The more we focus on Jesus, the more grateful—and life-giving— we become.

But often our focal point begins to shift. We allow the whispers of self to stifle God's voice, and we become motivated by other things—usually self—many times without recognizing it. We feel disappointed when we give, even if our impact on others is high. Our own needs scream for attention, and we are driven to give in order to fill ourselves up, or we pull back from giving altogether.

As I have talked with women, I've identified some common counterfeit motivations. If we want to become women of a generous spirit, we need to evaluate our motivations and exchange the counterfeit ones with life-giving ones.

MIXED MOTIVE #1: GIVING TO BE BLESSED

The actions of a woman who gives out of gratitude and one who gives to be blessed look deceptively similar. But one gives from fullness and the other gives in order to be filled.

When we give out of gratitude, we give out of our awareness of God's love and involvement in our lives. We enjoy life-giving interaction with him, the comfort of his presence, and the power of his Spirit. Our giving flows from our relationship with him. Our focus is on God—not the results of our giving.

However, when we give in order to be blessed, we give expecting positive life-circumstances. We believe in an implied spiritual formula that says: *If I do A, then B will happen. If I lead Bible studies, teach Sunday school, help with needs at church, serve on the mission field . . . God will bless me by granting my desires.*

When we do A, and B doesn't happen, we are disappointed. So what do we do? We just give more—but still nothing changes. The formula isn't working. We still feel empty. We don't even realize that our giving is self-focused instead of God-focused.

Liz, now in her early forties, reflects on her Christian upbringing, which unwittingly emphasized living by a formula. She had spent years giving to others with the unrecognized expectation that God would bless her with "the abundant life," which to her meant positive life-circumstances.

She told me, "I had a sincere desire to serve God and be obedient to him. I wanted to do the 'right' thing, find the 'right' answer, be the 'right' person. I worked hard at this. My trust in God was almost superstitious. In my heart I was afraid that if I didn't do those things, God would punish me. I thought that if God were happy with me, he would bless me with good things. When he didn't, I was hurt and frustrated. Not only did I lack some of the good things I wanted—a husband, a reputation for being godly, happiness—I didn't feel God's presence. I was confused by continuing messages I received from others that I was critical and judgmental. How could this be when I'd been a Christian all my life?"

Liz became increasingly disillusioned. She kept doing the "right" things—going to church, getting involved with Bible studies, discipling high school students, having daily devotions—yet her expectations about the Christian life didn't match her experience.

"I seemed to be doing all I was supposed to do, and it wasn't working. I was burned out and unhappy. I didn't even know it then, but I was very angry at God for not holding up his end of the bargain. I was lonely, hurt, confused, and very, very tired. It takes a lot of energy to constantly try to do the right thing! I was dead inside, and that scared me the most."

Liz's perspective began to change when she met some individuals who loved her unconditionally and invited her to talk about her questions and spiritual journey. They allowed her to be who she was without condemning her or pressuring her to change. Liz said, "I kept thinking they would be disappointed in me if I didn't make the choices I thought they wanted me to make—but it never happened. I slowly began to realize that God was the same way. He wanted the real me, not one I 'dressed up' in order to please him."

What Liz came to realize, in part, was that she had been trying to live by a formula that she believed would make God happy with her. She gave, not out of a sense of gratitude, but out of a sense of obligation and fear. She gave in order to get something in return— approval from God. She gave from an empty well that she believed would be filled when she performed correctly. Albeit unconsciously, *self* was at the center of her motivation.

Liz is in the process of focusing on her relationship with God in a personal and genuine way. "I'm still not sure what it means to be a servant," Liz reflects. "In the last five years, I've been changing my paradigm about God and faith. I'm moving from cookie-cutter Christianity to try to find out from God himself who he is. I still struggle with what difference God makes in my life, but I'm trying to live a genuine life before him."

In order to exchange a motivation of giving to be blessed for the motivation of gratitude, we must enter into a relationship with God in which we focus on knowing him better. The more we discover who he is for ourselves, the more we will be filled with love and gratitude.

When we give from fullness, we have more energy and enthusiasm. Remember how Liz talked about being worn out? That's a sure sign of giving with the wrong motivation. When we give out of gratitude, we will be generous spirits even when circumstances aren't as we hoped. We receive life from our relationship with God, not from positive circumstances.

MIXED MOTIVE #2: GIVING TO PLEASE OTHERS

When we give to please others, a great burden hangs on the response of the recipients of our giving. If they respond with appreciation and applause, we feel like our giving was worthwhile. If they respond with little or no enthusiasm, we feel like failures.

Again, self is at the center when we give in this manner. We want to be accepted and acknowledged by others for what we do.

While those feelings are normal, God desires us to look to him to meet those needs. Instead of trying to get something from our giving, we focus on him and receive all we need. When we come to God empty, he fills us in unexpected and supernatural ways. He may not change our circumstances; he may not answer our requests to our liking; he may not move other people in our lives to respond to us with love, but he will give us peace.

When we come to God with open and honest hearts, he reveals himself to us. If we come into his presence in order to see him, he transforms our desires from self-focused ones into the desire to know him better. As a result of just being with him for who he is, we are filled with his love and with gratitude. If we haven't experienced this love and gratitude, maybe self is still at the center of our lives.

Nan told me her whole life used to revolve around finding out what other people wanted from her and then trying to fill the bill. She depended on accolades for her efforts. If those accolades never arrived, Nan suffered deep disappointment and was emotionally drained for days.

One Sunday Nan volunteered to teach Sunday school. She admits to fantasizing about the response to her stepping forward to fill that gap. She envisioned a warm and spirited reply from the director of the Sunday school and continuing affirmation for her work.

Right from the beginning, Nan was disappointed. Her phone call to volunteer was met with mild appreciation. She began teaching without any fanfare and faithfully taught each week for a year.

One Sunday morning, all the teachers were recognized during the morning worship services. Nan enjoyed her moment of standing with several dozen other teachers but went home feeling let down.

Her reason for giving had been herself. She was giving to gain acceptance, appreciation, and applause. When her expectations weren't met, she felt empty. Nan resigned her position, weighted down by her own unacknowledged motivations.

Looking back, Nan sees that her giving had little life-giving power. She was tired and visibly unhappy much of the time. Her teaching lacked the vitality needed to keep the children interested, and they were often restless and bored. Nan grew irritated with their behavior and cheated herself of seeing them as young people who could be changed by her love.

Nan told me she is rethinking her motives for giving. She's taking a break from "doing" and is in the process of strengthening her relationship with God.

When we give to get, we are not life-givers. If we exchange our mixed motive for a godly motive, God can once again transform us into women of generous spirits. How can we make this exchange? Again, by focusing on God and getting to know him better. We exchange the belief that our value is based on the approval of others for a belief that our value comes from God.

MIXED MOTIVE #3: GIVING TO ACCOMPLISH OUR OWN AGENDAS

Perhaps the most obviously selfish motivation is giving to accomplish our own agendas. We try to manipulate circumstances by controlling the outcome of personal encounters. We become skilled at getting what we want and become self-reliant. We see people as a means to our ends. Often, when we are motivated this way, we give little and lose the desire to become generous women.

When I was a young girl, one such independent woman became my ideal. I watched her many times on film as she controlled her world with great flare. One scene in particular stands out.

Scarlett O'Hara, fiery heroine of the epic Civil War drama *Gone with the Wind*, lies helplessly doubled over in a barren field on her family's plantation. Her parents are dead, she and her remaining family have no food, and the taxes levied on her plantation by the victorious Yankees are due.

As if infused by some transforming elixir, the crumpled form on the screen begins to rise. With a clenched fist held high, Scarlett daringly declares to the heavens, "With God as my witness, I'll never be hungry again!"

"Yes!" I whispered. "Yes, I want to be like Scarlett O'Hara!"

I was eleven years old when I first saw *Gone with the Wind* and embraced the Scarlett-in-the-field as a role model.

I want to survive, overcome obstacles, clench my fist, and rise above my circumstances, I thought to myself as the houselights came up in the Ritz Theater, signaling intermission.

For three hours and fifty-two minutes, I bought the package of the attractively wrapped self-sufficient woman. Scarlett O'Hara may have been vicious, but she was never defeated. Down, perhaps, but not for long. With the help of no one, she manipulated her way through one tragedy after another.

Even as the camera rolled to a halt, Scarlett lifted her head triumphantly to declare with eye-shimmering hope that she would get Rhett Butler back—tomorrow. "For, after all, tomorrow is another day!"

When I watch *Gone with the Wind* now, I laugh at my girlish fascination with celluloid beauty and shallowness. But I understand my response. After all, the self-sufficient woman is in control. It doesn't matter how tough life gets, she will figure out a way to hold the reins. Self-empowerment is her goal. Fulfillment comes from exercising that power. Any act of generosity is only employed as it serves to meet her ends.

While I never wanted to be overbearing like Scarlett, I was intrigued with the idea of overcoming great odds by aggressively taking charge of my life.

When I was first widowed, I felt safe and protected. I enjoyed tremendous support and lived in a sheltered cocoon while adjusting to life without my husband. As time went on, however, I realized I was a vulnerable female in an unfriendly world, and I decided to take control of what I could. While I felt close to God, I also felt the need to be tough in the dailiness of life. Some of my friends commented on my burgeoning independence, and I tartly replied, "If my choices are open doors myself or have them hit me in the face, I'll open my own, thank you."

I remember the first time I went to buy a car. I took Lisa and Lara, ages eight and eleven years old, with me while I surveyed car lots. When I finally found a car I liked, I attracted the attention of a hungry salesman and followed him inside to "talk" about price. He told me the only way to determine the price was to evaluate the trade-in price for my current car. I surrendered my keys and waited while another man took my car for a ride.

An hour later, I was still trying to get my keys back. The salesman was engaging me in a battle of wills over what my car was worth. Lisa was sitting in a chair next to me, and Lara was playing on the floor in front of the salesman's desk. Finally, after many polite attempts to persuade him to give me back my keys, I abruptly stood up.

"Give me my keys, NOW!" I yelled.

Lisa jumped up beside me as I snatched the keys from the startled salesman. With an angry look of contempt, I turned and stormed away from his desk with the keys clutched tightly in my hand.

As we got close to the showroom door, Lisa whispered, "Mom, Lara is still back there on the floor."

I was aware that all eyes in the room were on me as I was making my grand exit. I couldn't stop and ruin my moment.

Without turning, I whispered back to Lisa, "GO GET HER!"

Lisa retrieved her unsuspecting sister, and I continued my walk of triumph to my car.

I felt exhilarated. That salesman had not worn down my resistance. I had gotten out of there without signing on any dotted line.

Why did I feel so good? Self-sufficiency brings a temporary high and can often affect circumstances. It is one of the world's most attractive alternatives to selflessness. It puts control at the center of life and wraps autonomy in a guise of euphoric existence. It seems to make sense. We think: *The world is a dangerous and hurtful place with everyone looking out for number one, so I'd better learn to look out for myself.*

However, self-sufficiency leads to coldness of heart and loneliness. Self-sufficiency can sometimes be effective in getting us what we want, but it is not a place to live. It denies pain by stuffing it under a veneer of hardness. It prevents us from giving and receiving love by pretending we don't need others. When we focus on accomplishing our own agendas, we view life with God very much on the periphery.

What would have been a life-giving response to the car salesman? He *was* trying to manipulate me. I don't think it would have been wise for me to succumb to his tactics and agree to buy a car for too high a price. But I could have treated him differently. I could have firmly requested my keys or politely asked to speak to someone else. I could have even communicated my awareness of what he was trying to do and my understanding that he was only doing his job.

My words could have been strong, but respectful. I could have given him truthfulness seasoned with kindness.

When we are convinced of our need for God, we give gratefully because God meets our needs. As we grow to know him better, we become more and more able to lay down our controlling ways and increase our dependence on him. We move toward seeing others as individuals instead of pawns in our game of life.

Our hearts begin to be touched; and in turn, we want to touch others.

READY FOR A CHANGE

Maybe you see yourself in one—or all—of these scenarios. Our motivations are complex and subject to our emotions. But if we are conscious of the need to change and aware of godly motivation, we are on our way to becoming life-giving women.

The following charts summarize the significant impact our motivations have on our ability to give, and the impact of giving out of gratitude. When you feel confused about why you are giving or disappointed with the results of your giving, refer back to these charts to help you untangle what your real motives may be.

MOTIVATIONS FOR GIVING/ IMPLICATIONS OF THOSE MOTIVATIONS

Motivation	To be blessed	To please others	To accomplish own agenda
Expectation	Positive circumstances	Appreciation, acceptance	Control

Life-giving impact on others	Medium to low	Low	Low
Life view	Formula Christianity works	Value comes from others	Self-sufficiency is best way to live
Results for giver	Disappointment	Disappointment	Independence, loneliness

GODLY MOTIVATION FOR BECOMING WOMEN OF A GENEROUS SPIRIT

Motivation	Gratitude overflowing, heart full of love
Expectation	Fulfilling relationship with God, regardless of circumstances
Life-giving impact on others	High
Life view	Life-giving love flows from fullness of relationship with God
Results for giver	Fruits of the Spirit

We don't exchange mixed motivations for godly motivations overnight. It's an ongoing process. Try not to be discouraged if you revert back to your old motives for giving and persevere in adjusting your perspective to giving out of gratitude.

Questions and Suggestions

1. Which of the women in the chapter resemble you? Explain. (There may be more than one.)

2. Write a paragraph that describes your primary motivation for giving. Your motivation may be one that isn't covered in this chapter.

3. How do you feel when you give and aren't appreciated? How do you respond to the person who was unappreciative?

4. Think about a time in your life when you have felt real gratitude. Write down how that sense of gratitude motivated you. Did you feel energized, eager to express your feelings, eager to give?

When Good Things Go Awry

When I began evaluating why I wasn't the giving woman I longed to be, I saw the need to make some adjustments in my life. My boundaries had become rigid, my life roles were changing, I was feeling insignificant, and I was overinvolved in activities. I was too busy—too tired—to give.

Setting boundaries, fulfilling specific roles, and being involved in activities are all positive behaviors, but they can get out of balance. If that happens, we don't need to "toss the baby out with the bathwater." We can make changes to bring those activities back into balance, keeping the positives and moderating the negatives. With awareness and commitment, we can maintain healthy boundaries, shift the focus of our giving when our roles change, and be responsible, involved women who are not exhausted by busyness.

WHEN BOUNDARIES BECOME RIGID

Many of us grew up without boundaries, and our spirits became damaged by people who took advantage of us. As a result, we have confused compliance with kindness. That's what happened to Anita.

Anita was sexually abused as a child. She was a loving and giving little girl who believed that she was supposed to be obedient and respectful to adults—even adults who hurt her. Although the abuse had stopped when she was a teenager, Anita had not learned how to establish boundaries to prevent abuse in the future, even as an adult.

She married and continued to be a compliant woman, trying to love and give whatever was asked of her. Then unresolved issues from her past began to cause tension in her marriage. She no longer enjoyed sexual relations with her husband and began to resent his pursuing her.

"I am the victim's victim," her husband said. "I feel sorry for her, but she is punishing me in the meantime."

Her husband convinced her to see a counselor to help her work through the pain of her past and establish healthy boundaries in her relationships. Anita learned to express her feelings honestly and to talk with her husband about her need to limit their sexual activity while she began the healing process.

For the first time in her life, Anita began to experience security and personal value. She realized that she didn't have to comply with her husband's wishes if she didn't want to. Anger that she had suppressed for years came spilling out. Her husband tried to be understanding and patient. However, over the next several years Anita continued to erect boundaries, and she withdrew from him more and more. She stopped fixing meals, accompanying him to social events, and talking openly with him. When he tried to draw her out, she would accuse him of being intrusive. Her boundaries had become too rigid, shutting out her husband almost completely. She went from giving away too much to giving nothing at all.

In their book *Boundaries,* Dr. Henry Cloud and Dr. John Townsend describe this phase of boundary setting as reactive and point out the need to move beyond it:

> *In reality, they [compliant people with no previous boundaries] had been complying for years, and their pent-up rage explodes. This reactive phase of boundary creation is helpful, especially for victims. They need to get out of the powerless, victimized place in which they may have been forced by physical and sexual abuse, or by emotional blackmail and manipulation. We should herald their emancipation.*
>
> *But when is enough enough? . . . It is crucial for victims of abuse to feel the rage and hatred of being powerless, but to be screaming "victim rights" for the rest of their lives is being stuck in a "victim mentality."[1]*

One day Anita looked in the mirror and saw a self-focused woman with little trace of a generous spirit. She realized that her boundaries needed to be more flexible with the people she could trust, otherwise she would be unable to have an emotionally intimate relationship.

Cloud and Townsend call flexible boundaries, *proactive boundaries.*

> *You must react to find your own boundaries, but having found them, you must "not use your freedom to indulge the sinful nature." Eventually, you must rejoin the human race you have reacted to, and establish connections as equals, loving your neighbor as yourself.*
>
> *This is the beginning of proactive, instead of reactive, boundaries. . . . Proactive people show what they love, what they want, what they purpose, and what they stand for. These people are very different from those who are known by what they hate, what they don't like, what they stand against, and what they will not do.[2]*

Anita found she could express her true self and be loving at the same time. She began to discover that loving others and giving to them is not synonymous with doing whatever they ask. Love is demonstrated in the context of living relationships where people talk, listen, forgive, respect, and care deeply for each other.

In time Anita adjusted her boundaries so that her husband could come back into her life, and she could reach out to him. She moved from a "victim mentality" to an active partnership with God in setting healthy boundaries. She and her husband both worked on putting God in the center of their relationship and viewing each other as God intended. As Anita focused on her relationship with God, she grew more and more generous, yet she was not damaged in the process. She knew when to say no and when to give.

FOCUS ON GOD, NOT SELF-PROTECTION

Sexual abuse is not the only reason we erect rigid boundaries to protect ourselves from pain; we can also withdraw behind boundaries because of a hurt that disillusioned us—even within the community of believers. A few years ago I attended a meeting of women in leadership from various churches. A number of them admitted that it was increasingly difficult to find women who would get involved in church ministry.

"A lot of women have been wounded inside a community where they expected to be safe," one leader said. "They have retreated and decided to stay uninvolved to protect themselves."

As I listened, I remembered my own long-ago decision to be a lone-ranger Christian. "I will never be actively involved in a church again," I had said to anyone who would listen. My attitude was a result of a vitriolic split in leadership in a church where I been active for a number of years. I was shocked when the conflict resulted in spiritual brothers and sisters hurting each other, and I contributed to the melee, hurling insults and delivering verbal punches. I hurt others, and I myself was deeply wounded.

Finally I walked away, both literally and figuratively. When my daughters and I moved, I also packed my emotional bags and built a wall around my heart. I decided to worship God as a pew-sitter but never again as a participant in any institutionalized religious organization. I still wanted to give, but I thought I could give from behind a wall.

The emptiness was much more painful than I expected, and after about a year, I concluded I couldn't be a generous woman when I was focused on not being hurt by others. The reentry and continuing vulnerability hasn't always been easy. It is a process that involves much of what is written in this book.

I want to be a woman of a generous spirit. Such women are defined by what is at their core, enabling them not only to adjust their boundaries, but also their focus when their life roles change.

WHEN LIFE ROLES CHANGE

The women's Bible study group sat in a casual circle in Irene's living room. Six women in their early fifties had decided to meet for mutual encouragement as they faced some of midlife's trying issues.

After meeting for several weeks, Irene talked about her growing feelings of uselessness. "I just don't feel like anyone needs me," she confessed. "My kids are grown, and my husband is still engrossed in his job. A lot of my friends have gone to work, and I just don't feel significant."

"I know," Bonnie agreed. "Just the other day I found myself wishing the kids were little again. How ironic when I used to long for time to myself. Sometimes I like the freedom, but I miss feeling needed."

Many women enjoy tremendous satisfaction by performing certain roles well. These roles are often the vehicles for releasing the overflow of God's love in our lives. When these roles change, however, our feelings of significance may plummet. We may find ourselves feeling empty and our spirits unable to muster up true generosity.

When roles change, it's normal to experience loss, but we don't always expect it.

I never dreamed that I would have difficulty shifting gears from my role as a parent of children to my role as a parent of adults. I spent several years fumbling around, trying to regain my perspective that God had a purpose for me. I felt like I had nothing substantial to give to others. Intellectually I knew that wasn't true, but that was how I felt.

When I gave myself some space to hear God, my sense of value began to be restored. I released myself from the pressure of thinking

I had to be busy every minute. I began to spend more time with God and to ask more specifically what kind of woman he wanted me to be. His answer didn't come in a thunderbolt, but I began to see opportunities for giving to others.

Our Bible study spent the next year meeting as a support group for each other. We talked about our adjustments to change, shared articles and books on related topics, questioned and listened to each other, prayed and cried together, sought relationships with God, and gave each other encouragement. We slowed down in order to adjust to the changes in our lives.

At the end of the year, all of us felt we had moved through the most painful part of the transition. We had exchanged our conclusion that life was over when our roles as mothers ended for the truth that God infuses new life into each of us, regardless of age and performance.

Every woman will experience a variety of role changes throughout her life as a result of divorce, death of a loved one, job loss, health issues, geographical moves, parents and children growing older, or growing older ourselves. When change occurs, we need time to adjust to new ways of giving. As we focus on our relationship with God, he comes and fills in the gaps with his love. He helps us adapt to losses—even good ones—and allows us to see new directions for our giving.

Sometimes, though, those who want to be life-givers struggle with another thief: busyness.

WHEN WE *MUST* BE BUSY

A few years ago my husband, Steve, and I were enjoying a vacation in Europe with another couple. We had traded in our accumulated mileage for free tickets and jetted off for three weeks in France, Switzerland, and Italy.

Our first stop was Paris, which is a bustling whirl of activity day and night. We filled every moment of our four days there.

On the fifth morning, we packed our van and headed for Switzerland. After a scenic drive through the French countryside, we arrived at a small town bordering Lake Geneva. Our bed-and-breakfast overlooked the lake. We oohed and aahed at the sight of such peaceful surroundings after the hustle of Paris. But sighs of delight had barely escaped my lips, when I shifted gears. My companions hadn't joined my instantaneous redirection and looked surprised when I announced, "I'm off!"

Steve was used to my abrupt change of pace and just smiled. I walked expectantly down the hill and toward the main street of the town. It was about 1:00 P.M. As I came to the first corner of the shopping area, I noticed that the streets were relatively deserted.

A sign on the door of the first shop I approached explained the lack of foot traffic. *Closed from noon until three.* I tried the doorknob anyway, but it was locked. I jiggled it as if there were some mistake. Frustrated, I went to the next shop. The same sign in this store window was delicately embroidered in needlepoint, but I didn't appreciate the artistic touch. I was irritated that my plan had been thwarted.

I walked back to the hotel to snatch Steve from whatever cozy chair he had settled into, only to find him in our room asleep. Our friends were nowhere to be found, and I could only assume that they, too, were resting.

I didn't want to go to sleep! I didn't want to read! I wanted to be out and about *doing something!* I walked down to the living room, out on the patio, around the house, and back to our room. Steve was still sleeping.

I finally sat in one of the chairs in the library, put my feet up on a stool, and laid my head back. One of my favorite Rachmaninoff melodies was lilting from the CD player. After a few moments, it occurred to me that the stillness was pleasant. The tension in my body began to drain away. The breeze off the lake drifted through the open French doors and carried with it the scent of lilac. *Why don't I do this more often?* I asked myself.

There was an almost audible response: *You are addicted to busyness.*

My reverie was broken as I sat up with a start and walked out onto the balcony.

When I was home, I was always complaining about being too busy. Everyone I knew did. I had tried countless times to conquer the clock with little success. But as I stood on the balcony of that lovely bed-and-breakfast, I realized I didn't take advantage of the opportunities that fell into my lap. I often felt I was wasting time if I wasn't active. While that sounds responsible, the truth is that busyness often shouts over the soft whisper of God's voice. It's impossible to focus on him—or others—when we are always rushing from one thing to the next. Here I had an opportunity to stop my activity, and I didn't want to!

I'm not alone in this struggle. "Busyness is a curse," Sandy told me. "I think it is something that can pull us off the road, and we get stuck. At our last women's breakfast, we talked about keeping our hearts aflame on the road of following Jesus. Psalm 51:12 says, 'Restore to me the joy of your salvation and grant me a willing spirit, to sustain me.' " Sandy went on to say that the busyness of life robs us of time to have our spirits sustained, to give God room to fill us up.

Jan breathed out a long, slow laugh when I asked her about busyness. "I think that as I get busier with stuff to do—at church, school, with kids—I forget to focus on the joy. Joy like we had when we were children, skipping down a street. We need to keep ourselves centered on the joy that Christ can give. That's the challenge that busyness gives us. How do we maintain the relationship with Christ to be able to deal with the interruptions of life?"

There is an old Irish saying: "When God made time, he made plenty of it." Busy women rarely need more time. Rather, we need to alter our belief that we can't change. We need to bring balance back to our lives—or establish it for the first time.

Many of us are addicted to activity. We fill up every moment.

Oh, we love to collapse in a chair with a magazine or watch mindless television to unwind. But the routine pace of our life is frantic. Have we become so accustomed to the busy status quo that we don't stop and reflect about how we really want to live? Are we trapped in jobs that drain the life out of us? Do we say yes to too many things?

We can only reflect on questions like these during snippets of stillness. The view from that balcony several years ago was the beginning of intentional little changes in my choices. I certainly haven't conquered the curse of busyness, but I am making progress.

The following chart summarizes the critical points of the out-of-balance positives we've looked at:

POSITIVES THAT CAN HINDER

Influence	Hindered by focus on self-protection	Interrupted by changing roles	Stifled by busyness
Expectation	Safety	Expectation is difficult to predict	Someday things will change
Life view	Boundaries keep safe	May be focused on God, but feel like value comes from specific roles	Busyness is unavoidable
Results for person	Fear, skepticism, lack of giving	Surprised by feelings of insignificance	Fragmentation, frustration, feeling trapped

Is It Time for a Change?

Making adjustments in any one of these areas may seem overwhelming. You may have labored to establish boundaries and now realize you need to draw different lines. You may have functioned for many years in particular roles that are no longer applicable, and you find yourself dealing with unexpected emotions. Or the busyness of life may have a strangling grip on you. Remember: Change begins with awareness. But if you and I want to become generous women, we can risk making adjustments that previously might have seemed far-fetched.

Questions and Suggestions

1. Describe how you use boundaries in your life. Do you feel they are rigid or flexible? Do you need to establish some new ones?

2. What are some ways you can begin to flex your boundaries? Write down your thoughts and meet with God. Ask him to fill you with his love and confidence to begin to make adjustments in those boundaries.

3. If you have recently experienced a significant role change in your life, invite a few women friends who are in similar circumstances to meet with you and talk together about this transition time. Think about becoming a support group for each other.

4. Do you feel overwhelmed by the busyness of life?

5. Schedule a few small amounts of time (ten minutes) to think about changes you want to make to better handle busyness. Write down your thoughts.

6. Think and pray about making adjustments in your schedule to free you from some of the stress of busyness.

7. Meet with a friend and talk through how to think about—and adjust to—busyness.

Chapter 4

Healing Wounds, Relieving Tensions

Jesus became a servant—a giver—in the most sacrificial way. He gave his very life on our behalf. When we commit to follow him, we are to be generous women who, in humility, serve others. Paul wrote in his letter to the Philippians that we should have the same attitude that Christ had:

> *Your attitude should be the same as that of Christ Jesus:*
> *Who, being in very nature God,*
> *did not consider equality with God something to be grasped,*
> *but made himself nothing,*
> *taking the very nature of a servant,*
> *being made in human likeness.*
> *And being found in appearance as a man,*

he humbled himself and became obedient to death—even death on a cross! (Philippians 2:5-8)

This kind of giving brings with it some tensions.

We hear God tell us to be selfless, but we fear that our unselfishness will deplete us. We are pulled between our desire to give and our need to receive.

We wrestle with hurts and disappointments. We want to give but in ways that don't damage us, and we aren't sure how. We want to trust God to meet our needs, but doubts fill our minds. How can we follow, give, and trust a God who sometimes seems distant or unresponsive?

Giving God's way—out of gratitude—is dependent on our trusting him. We can't experience feelings of gratitude for what we've received if we doubt the Giver.

WHAT IS GOD *REALLY* SAYING?

In order to relieve some of these tensions, we need to evaluate if we are really hearing God or if his voice is being obscured. Are we carrying unhealed wounds that cause us to think that giving will always be painful? Are we trusting God enough to follow him without reservation?

One day I was driving to a nearby lake with my grandson Justin so he could feed the ducks who had taken up permanent residence there. He was sitting in his car seat in the backseat of my car, and I had the rearview mirror positioned so I could see his face.

At two years old, he was fascinated with trying to repeat everything he heard. I looked at him in the mirror and said, "Justin, after we feed the ducks, we're going to the Heidelberg for lunch."

The Heidelberg is a German restaurant here in Colorado Springs with lively music and an ambiance that I thought he'd think was fun. He looked up at me in the mirror and slowly pronounced the word *heidel-bird*.

I smiled and praised him for the near-perfect repetition of a complex word. For the rest of our ride to the lake, he kept repeating *heidel-bird* over and over again. When we arrived and parked the car, his attention turned to finding the ducks.

We walked around the lake and came upon several of his feathered friends basking on the bank in the morning sun. Justin walked closer to them, leaned over, and said loud and clear, "Hi, del birds!"

I had known that he didn't understand the meaning of the word, but I laughed at Justin's association of the restaurant name with words he did know. *Heidelberg* and *Hi bird* sounded the same to him. He connected the meaning of a familiar phrase to his understanding of another similar-sounding word.

We often do the same: We attach meaning to what we hear God say through the filter of our associations.

I used to hear the word *selfless* and automatically think "doormat." Some previous teaching I'd received implied that being selfless meant allowing others to take advantage of me. I was to keep quiet, be compliant, and give whenever I was asked in whatever ways were needed. I soon found myself burned-out and resentful. So when I would hear the word *selfless*, I understood it through the filter of my negative experience. God's voice was obscured by the painful memory of saying yes to every request.

Then I began to look at women of a generous spirit. I realized that they understand God's command to be selfless in a different way than I had. They often say no to requests but continue to be life-givers. They decline with kindness, confidence, and grace. They don't resent being asked to do things but feel the freedom to choose for themselves what they think God would have them do.

I wondered, *What is God really saying when he asks us to die to self? How could I do that and not feel used?* I knew I had to take time to sit down with him and reflect on what he might mean. I had to spill out my feelings to him and pray and wait. I had to learn to bridle any spontaneous yes and wait for God to guide me.

In time my thinking changed. I no longer felt guilty for being limited or saying no. I asked him to show me what being selfless means. I spilled my feelings to him and prayed and waited. I controlled any spontaneous yes to requests and brought those requests before God. I answered only when I had reflected and prayed about the decision.

The Holy Spirit has the power to change us if we allow him. That change is not an event but a process. And the first step in that process is becoming aware of biblical words or phrases that trigger painful associations. Then we need to face the residual damage from those past hurts.

Before I could respond positively to the idea of being a woman of a generous spirit, I had to work through my woundedness. Once I healed, I became better able to hear those trigger words from God's perspective.

Many of us have other issues that need God's healing touch before we can really hear his intended message for us.

I COULDN'T *NOT* GIVE BACK

Traci's story is not unusual. She wanted to give back to God out of a heart full of gratitude, but soon found hurts in her life screaming for attention.

"The year I became a Christian I ran away from home. That's how I found Jesus," Traci told me with a calm spirit, which testifies to the healing power operating in her life.

"From age fifteen to twenty-five, I was trying to perform for God, trying to give back to God. That's the message I got—'Give out of gratitude.' It shifted into obligation and then denial that I wasn't equipped to save the world. I had tons of stuff I needed to deal with, but nobody asked what was going on at home. Nobody knew that the year I became a Christian I ran away from home.

"Since the end result was that I found God, all seemed okay. I spent ten years believing that getting saved was enough, and I could wipe out whatever happened. I was giving out of a tremendously wounded spirit."

Traci talked about her continued attempts to pay God back. She was grateful for her salvation and was skilled at hiding behind a mask of competency. But underneath, she realized she was emotionally unhealthy. Life wasn't working.

"The panic was rising, so I started therapy. My therapist recommended joining a women's therapy group, which was my turnaround. As far as I can remember, it was the first setting in which I had been completely real and honest about my limitations and brokenness. Something happened in there when I stopped trying to perform and was given permission to be myself.

"During those few years I pulled back. I had been so involved in so many people's lives, and I stopped that. I started to get my needs met. I had no sense of God being a nurturing God. My image was that he was a king and I was a servant, and it didn't have a lot to do with love."

Traci's healing process stripped her of the illusion that she could live with a facade. She came to the humbling and freeing reality of who she really is. "I've had to look at this save-the-world mentality I had. I needed to be all things to all people all the time. But I can't do that. I am just one among many, and I am called to live humbly among my fellow human beings and give back—stripped of pretense and giving from a real place.

"I needed to find a place in myself that was not only broken but that had received a huge healing from God. Once I actually let some of those needs be met, I was no longer desperate or looking for healing anymore in what I did."

Traci is a beautifully full and giving woman. She no longer manufactures giving to fit the expectations of others. She gives from the security of knowing who she is and experiencing the healing power of God in her life.

One of her expressions of gratitude is demonstrated in work she does as a Court Appointed Special Advocate for Abused Children (CASA) volunteer. "Because of the gratitude for what I have experienced, I have a passion for giving kids a little of what I desperately needed—a little bit of respect, a little bit of love. I got into CASA for the right reasons. I give from a deep healing place inside of me. I want to give what I have received."

"When I think of women of a generous spirit, I think of Traci," her friend Liz said.

"She is involved with CASA as a result of an intentional decision to give back. She saw it would be shortsighted to stop with her healing. I saw her go beyond her comfort zone and give, motivated out of conviction."

"The key," Traci smiled as she spoke, "in genuine generosity is giving from a broken heart that has been touched by the grace of God. It compels you to give back. I couldn't *not* give back."

Traci's giving did not come easily. But she has moved through the healing process, engaged in a renewed relationship with God, and is learning to trust him again to sustain her when the tension of living by faith challenges her confidence.

Spiritual and emotional healing is a complex and often difficult process. If neglected, however, our ability to hear God and give from fullness will be inhibited.

When we suffer physical illness, we are acutely aware of the need for healing. Painful symptoms drive us to the doctor's office for help. Our quality of life is impaired unless we subject ourselves to the physician's prescriptions, even if treatment means interruption of our routine.

You may find yourself in need of God's healing touch, or you may be in the middle of a healing process right now. Friends, counselors, support groups, and doctors may all be participants in God's plan to renew you. As your heart responds to him, your transformed wounds will be planted in fertile ground where God can nurture and grow your faith. He can fill you and give you the desire to give out of that fullness.

But before we can become selfless, we need to move beyond healing to trusting God again. We may flinch because we have always connected the presence of trust with the absence of tension. Renewed thinking and healed hearts can help us reconcile one of the greatest tensions believers face.

DOES TRUST IN GOD MEAN LACK OF TENSIONS?

Why does God allow bad things to happen to good people? Many have wrestled with this question. Whether it's because we simply want it to be true or because we have been taught it's true, we hang on to the idea that trusting God means he will solve all our problems and life will be good and pain free. When that doesn't happen, we often doubt God.

Norman Mailer, in his novel *The Gospel According to the Son*, attempts to resolve the tension between Christianity's claims about God's goodness and power and the pain in the world by concluding that God is an imperfect deity.

In a review of Mailer's book, Margaria Fichtner writes,

> *In a world of holocausts and gulags, bombings, and repression, false profits and false prophets, Mailer says, "I began to wonder, Well, what kind of God do we have?, and it seemed to me that the only answer was an imperfect one. . . . The feeling I have is that philosophy has to come to a full stop if God is all-perfect, because the history of the 20th century suggests that there's something terribly wrong and loose in the universe. . . . If God is all-powerful, then God cannot be all good. If God is all good, then God—he or she—cannot be all-powerful."* [1]

Before we toss Mr. Mailer's premise in the heretic file, let's face the challenge his words present to those of us who do believe in an all-good, all-powerful God. If we are honest, we will admit to our own discomfort with the presence of evil in a world controlled by God. When we try to reason why he allows pain and suffering, we project our ways of thinking onto the way we think God should reason.

We do this all the time in our relationships with each other. When Steve and I have a disagreement and his behavior is something other than what I desire, I immediately think, *If that were me, I would act differently.*

Steve, an introvert, usually withdraws when we have a conflict. He needs time to mull over the implications of various resolutions. Then he calmly reappears to discuss his thoughts. I, on the other hand, respond to conflict with instantaneous verbiage. I want to talk, NOW! As an extrovert, I often view his withdrawal as disinterest, and I wonder how he can act that way if he loves me. I assume he has moved on to more pressing issues and just doesn't care about me. But I'm wrong. I've learned that I project onto Steve what I would do if I were him. I am not him. He does love me—and he does withdraw. I have even grown to understand that this is what Steve does, but I still don't understand why he finds that preferable to talking immediately. I am limited in my ability to crawl inside his mind and view life from his perspective.

If we have difficulty figuring out why other *people* think and act the way they do, how much more trouble will we have when projecting our suppositions onto *God?* We say to ourselves, *If I were God, I would do things differently,* implying that we know better what we need than he does.

We wrestle with the tension of trusting a God whose ways often don't make sense to us. Mailer is right that "there's something terribly wrong and loose in the universe," but his conclusion that God is imperfect projects onto God our human standard of reason. Human reasoning untouched by the Holy Spirit concludes that God's goodness and/or power is equated with the elimination of things not-good—holocausts, gulags, bombings, repression, and personal pain in our lives and in the lives of those we love. That's what we, in our own perceived goodness, would do if we had the power.

Mailer, and many like him, seem to hold to a philosophy that demands that God's workings conform to a twisted logic: *If I can't understand why God does what he does, then what he does must be flawed.*

Scripture repeatedly tells us to abandon our own understanding and accept God's direction; "Trust in the LORD with all your heart and lean not on your own understanding; in all your ways acknowledge him, and he will make your paths straight" (Proverbs 3:5-6).

Our own understanding is limited, a humbling concept which we resist with the gears of our intellect engaged at peak performance. We, as human beings, control so much. Our knowledge of the world and our ability to manipulate it grow with every stroke of a computer keyboard. But we cannot leash the evil in the universe or eliminate personal pain in our own lives. The mind untouched by the Holy Spirit cannot acknowledge an all-powerful God existing simultaneously with that evil and pain.

Leslie Williams, in her book *Night Wrestling*, looks at how we all struggle with fear and confusion when pain touches our lives. Williams describes how she would get up out of bed at night and wrestle with God on the living room couch. Here she finally came to the point, in all things, of trusting God. She writes:

> *At some point on my couch in Houston, I accepted the fact that God was trustworthy. True, the only father-pattern I had was not ideal, but I finally bought the idea that God isn't like that. At first, this insight was an idea. It wasn't a feeling. Then, as I asked repeatedly for God to chisel a path from my brain to my heart, gradually, gradually, I allowed myself to relax the white-knuckled grip I had on my desire to control my life.[2]*

Gradually, gradually. The process of learning to trust cannot be hurried.

But trust we can. Amy Carmichael wrote of loving and trusting God so much that we quickly shut the door on self as soon as it begins to open: "If, the moment I am conscious of the shadow of self crossing my threshold, I do not shut the door, and in the power of Him who works in us to will and to do, keep that door shut, then I know nothing of Calvary love."[3]

Gradually relax, quickly shut.

Follow him, live with pain.

Live with tension.

Until we trust God, we will be unable to shut the door on self. And shutting the door on self is intrinsic to the Christian life. Becoming a woman who selflessly touches others isn't just a desirable ideal, it is a command laced through all of the teachings of Jesus. We are called to follow him and seek to be like him, to be his representatives in the world, to treat others with an amazing love that will draw them to God.

We assume the posture of trust at the foot of the cross. At the cross we all began our Christian walk, and we must continually return there. At the cross, with our faces in the dust and our hands clinging to a crudely splintered post, we receive the seeds of faith that empower us to live in the midst of tension with unexplainable joy. We are able to loosen our grip and struggle to our feet, wrapping ourselves around the evidence of an incomprehensible reality: God loves us in spite of the "something terribly wrong and loose" in each of us.

At the cross, we are forgiven. God's supernatural presence permeates our personal universes where the terrible wrongness used to reign.

We are able to unwrap ourselves from Calvary and go live, imperfectly, as the One on the cross directs. Evil is still loose in the world, but as we glance back over our shoulders at what God has done for us, our need to know why he works as he does lessens. When pain pierces us again, we are faced with a choice: Succumb to the faulty logic of the world, or run to the cross and bolster our trust.

The tension between trusting God and trusting reason tugs at us. Sometimes we linger at the edge of the shadow of the cross. We straddle a chasm of indecision—should I trust God again? Only when we bring our fear to the cross, do we receive God's power. "For the message of the cross is foolishness to those who are perishing, but to us who are being saved it is the power of God" (1 Corinthians 1:18).

We are creatures of habit, and some of us have been thinking the same way for years. We think we hear God, but in reality we have understood him through the filter of our own experience. We believe that we can give with unresolved hurts remaining unaddressed. We think we are grateful, but a closer look shows we doubt God's goodness.

But if we depend on him, God can help us live by faith—even amid the paradoxes we face. Tension still exists, but it need not rob us of faith or prevent us from becoming women of generous spirits.

Questions and Suggestions

1. What was your response when you read the quote by Amy Carmichael: *If, the moment I am conscious of the shadow of self crossing the threshold, I do not shut the door, and in the power of Him who works in us to will and to do, keep that door shut, then I know nothing of Calvary love.*

2. Are any of the words or phrases from that quote connected to negative conclusions you have already made? Write down those words and the feelings they reveal.

3. Are you aware of the need for healing from past hurts in your life? If so, determine to begin to get help for the process of healing. Call a trusted friend, pastor, or counselor and talk to him or her.

4. Write how you feel about trusting God and living with the tension of pain at the same time.

5. Spend some time in a quiet place thinking about your first encounter with Christ and your feelings of first love.

6. When you feel discouraged about becoming a woman of a generous spirit, return to thinking about that first love encounter again.

7. If you are ready, make a commitment to read this book in the context of pursuing your relationship with Jesus.

Read, think, reflect, make changes slowly.

If you are not ready, what is holding you back?

Pray that God will reveal to you what he would have you do.

8. If you are ready, enjoy the adventure!

Chapter 5

The Need to Forgive

I had to place my father in a nursing home around his eighty-fifth birthday. His dementia had made it impossible for him to care for himself. He was only there a short time, however, before he became combative and unwilling to take his medication. The day he swung his walking cane at the attendants trying to calm him, they decided to transfer him to the state hospital.

I visited him every week. The men's dormitory was off-limits to visitors, so I would watch for his frail figure to emerge from the dormitory door. He always greeted me with an enthusiastic smile and immediate recognition. "Oh Lois, darling, you're here!" he would say as his bony fingers wrapped around my face and he kissed my forehead.

The patients' lounge was noisy and full of other patients. All of these older men and women suffered from mental illness combined with potentially destructive behavior. It was not uncommon for a physical disturbance to break out.

My father had calmed considerably since his arrival at the hospital, so the nurse allowed me to sit with him on a bench in the entrance hall. The sound of the heavy, metal door latching behind us was a poignant reminder of where my father now lived. For many weekly visits during his three-month stay at the state hospital, my father and I would sit on that bench and talk. He was docile and teary, constantly wondering where my deceased mother was.

On one particular visit, he began to talk as if he were a boy—not in a child's voice, but an adolescent's. "You know, if Mother finds us, she'll beat me," he said, looking furtively from one side to the other.

"What do you mean, Daddy?" I asked. I thought he was referring to my own mother, who would never have caused him to be afraid.

"I mean . . . she'll beat me or BURN me!"

I realized he was talking about his mother. He thought I was a childhood friend named Lorraine. He told me that when his mother got mad, she burned him with cigarettes or with an iron. Tears rolled down his wrinkled cheeks as he told me things I'd never heard before. My father had never made disparaging remarks about his mother. He was an only child and talked like he had been spoiled and doted on. My grandmother had died when I was young, and in my memory she was cold and distant.

That day my father poured out a lifetime of fear and pain. He wept and unleashed more than eighty years of secrets. He had been repeatedly beaten by his mother and father. They had been, at once, praising and demeaning. He was given material gifts and received physical beatings for menial rule infractions.

All of my life my father had been a consummately angry man. We had endured a difficult relationship that revolved around his anger. Finally, I knew the source of it.

After my father's confession, he began to change. At the age of eighty-five and in the grip of irreversibly damaging illness, he began to forgive and heal. He was unable to articulate what was happening to him, but he changed. He was discharged from the state hospital and into a psychiatric nursing home, where he became the darling of the staff. His sarcasm was transformed into good-natured humor, and he showered compliments on the most disheveled co-patients.

I watched him with sadness and gratitude. His life could have been so different if he had resolved his anger years before. But I was grateful to see him roll around in his wheelchair with the freedom that comes with healing and forgiveness. Even though the people my father forgave were long dead, those of us who were near him benefited from this change in him.

In order to be generous and giving women, you and I need to release others—and ourselves—from being hostages of our anger and bitterness; we need to forgive. But to do this, we may need to look in the mirror for traces of anger and then release others from the penalty boxes we've kept them in.

OUR PRIVATE VIDEOTAPES

Anger is a thief. It robs us of joy and the ability to receive and give. Many of us need to forgive those who have hurt us in the past as well as learn to forgive others in the present.

Jill had been married to Daniel for over ten years when Daniel's son, Tom, graduated from college. During those ten years, the relationship between Jill and Tom had been strained. Tom was understandably hurt by his parents' divorce and had a tough time accepting his father's remarriage.

As Tom's graduation approached, Jill's apprehension grew. She was worried that she would be excluded from certain festivities and wondered if she would even be seated with Daniel at the dinner party following the graduation ceremony. Jill understood the preferential position of Tom's mother on this significant day, but she couldn't squelch her own worries about being left out.

I attended the graduation without any knowledge of Jill's concerns. After the ceremony, we all drove over to the country club where the reception was being held. The tables for the sit-down dinner sparkled with mirror-based centerpieces and crystal goblets. Filigrees of spring flowers filled the room with soft color and the subtle scent of a garden. It was truly an elegant affair.

I saw Jill seated next to Daniel at the family's table, smiling guiltily. "You look like the cat who swallowed the canary," I whispered as I pulled up a chair to sit by her.

She laughed quietly and said, "You wouldn't believe what I was going to do."

I had no idea what she was talking about but urged her to tell me.

"I was so sure that Daniel would neglect me today and so sure that Tom would snub me that I planned a grand exit," she confessed in whispered tones.

"What do you mean?"

"Not a disruptive exit, just one for Daniel's benefit. I assumed that I would not be seated at the family table, so I packed a suitcase and put it in the trunk of the car without Daniel knowing. I was going to pull him aside after the graduation exercises and dramatically ride off into the sunset with my bag packed."

"Are you kidding me?"

"I am so good at running scenarios through my mind about how I'll get people back if they hurt me. This time I really got carried away." She shook her head at her own deviousness as she talked.

While Jill's action may seem extreme, we are all subject to picturing academy-award-winning performances through our mental projectors. We fantasize revenge in glowing color and digital sound. When we do, self moves into first place and obliterates any thoughts of being filled by God and giving to others.

The temptation to take an offense and turn it into a triumph of wit and will is seductive. But this is the opposite of forgiveness. We can't fill our minds with life-giving thoughts *and* negative videotapes.

RENEWED THOUGHTS TOWARD OFFENDERS

Forgiveness often involves a complex and lengthy process that may require the help of a professional counselor, particularly in cases of abuse, but many times we harbor resentment for lesser offenses. It's impossible to live in this world and not get jostled, interrupted, misunderstood, neglected, and hurt in a myriad of ways.

When someone hurts me, my initial response is sarcasm. Alacrity of tongue brings high regard in many arenas of today's culture, but it is not consistent with following Jesus. I've learned that it helps to take the offense to God first, rather than to retaliate. In his presence, I can calm down and temper my reaction with God's spirit. "Bear with each other and forgive whatever grievances you may have against one another. Forgive as the Lord forgave you" (Colossians 3:13).

The Lord forgave us completely, and he paid the price for our offense. We need to abandon our fantasies of brilliant revenge and replace them with memories of God's forgiveness toward us. As we do, our thoughts change, and our hearts begin to soften.

Jill told me that as she unpacked her suitcase the night of Tom's graduation, she came face to face with her unwillingness to forgive. She had been hurt by Tom's response over the years and had been angry at Daniel for not more readily defending her.

Jill brought her feelings about Tom to God. Soon her thoughts changed, and her heart grieved over the pain Tom suffered as a result of his parents' divorce. Jill began to talk openly with Daniel, and together they sought counseling to address buried hurts from their past. They began to enjoy more security in their relationship and an improved ability to handle offenses as they occurred.

But such a happy ending is not always the case. Forgiveness is not always accompanied by improved relationships. Sara is divorced from her husband of over fourteen years. During her marriage she forgave repeated episodes of adultery and finally decided to end their marriage when Jerry refused to seek help and to change his ways. He willingly accepted her decision and continued his philandering.

Sara has a spirit of forgiveness. She worked through her hurt and bitterness over years of lies and was able to release her animosity toward Jerry. She still carries great sadness over the breakup of her marriage but also realizes that an unforgiving attitude toward Jerry would only rob her of healing.

A MATTER BETWEEN US AND GOD

It's one thing to forgive those who ask for forgiveness and seek to make amends for their offenses; it's another to forgive those who deny their offense—and even more, those who continue to hurt us.

There are a few people whom I say I have forgiven, but the bile of revenge gurgles up at the mention of their names. These few deny they have done anything offensive and invalidate the feelings of others, including my own. Confrontations have resulted in more denial. I know I must forgive them apart from their involvement. Together with God, I can forgive those who continue to offend or hurt me.

When the offending person won't admit to inflicting any hurt, forgiveness becomes a matter between us and God. We can ask for his supernatural intervention in our thinking and for his love to transform our anger into forgiveness. To forgive we don't need to remain in the physical presence of those who hurt us, but we do need to examine our attitudes toward them. In time, as we continue to struggle with our feelings in God's presence, he can change our hearts.

In order to resist the temptation to drop a word, convey a look, or breathe a sigh of condemnation against one of these people, we must continually come back into God's presence with our own pain.

Author and speaker Jackie Kendall suggests intentionally praying for the well-being of those we find difficult to forgive. I have started to do that and have found that I more frequently silence my tongue than when I didn't pray for them.

Forgiveness comes from a heart touched by God, a heart able to grow loving thoughts out of hurt feelings. Only the giver and God know if forgiveness is genuine. If we have not truly forgiven others, unkind thoughts will leap to life when we think about them. If we have forgiven them, our minds will rest in the presence of accepting, loving thoughts. Our desire for their hurt, our delight at their misfortune, will have faded away.

LIFE-GIVING POWER

Forgiving actions bring life. Even if it doesn't result in healed relationships, forgiveness brings life to the forgiver. Damaging and draining thoughts die in the presence of love. And often authentic forgiveness brings a life-giving touch to the offender. She is given the opportunity to reenter a relationship with someone she has hurt and to experience love in spite of her actions.

Women of a generous spirit don't carry grudges. They don't fantasize about getting even with people who hurt them. They acknowledge their true feelings to themselves and to God and to the offending person, but they don't get bent out of shape if the offender doesn't respond as they'd hoped.

They forgive, even if they are met with rudeness and more unkindness. Because generous women focus on God, their concern is how God wants them to think. He calls them—and all of us—to be forgiving.

When generous women bump into those who have hurt them, they are gracious and kind. They resist the temptation to throw out a sarcastic remark or turn the other way. They set and keep healthy boundaries that help protect them from repeat offenders, but they relate from within those boundaries with God's love. They speak respectfully and listen with care. They respond to questions honestly but lovingly. While their boundaries may not allow them to become deeply involved with people who hurt them, they still show them kindness. Sometimes that kindness brings others to an awareness of their own need to ask for forgiveness. Either way, women of a generous spirit forgive others.

Forgiveness frees us to love, to be filled by God's goodness, and to give generously to others.

Questions and Suggestions

1. Write down any feelings of anger you harbor toward others.

2. Make a commitment to stop running mental videotapes on how to get even.

3. Purposely replace those thoughts with prayer for those people and engagement with God about how you feel toward them.

4. Make a list of people you need to go to and offer the gift of forgiveness. Determine what that looks like with each individual, and begin to offer that gift. It may be a change in the way you greet them the next time you see them. It may be a kind word, a note, a lunch together. Or it may simply be to remember to pray for them and say nothing.

Chapter 6

How Can I Give and Not Feel Drained?

I've often been accused of inhaling my food. Steve, on the other hand, leisurely savors every bite and finishes a meal long after I have cleaned my plate. He eats less than I do but is satisfied longer. We sit at the table for the same amount of time and eat the same food, yet he receives more benefit from his meal than I do. His sense of fullness lasts longer than mine, and he experiences fewer cravings for unhealthy foods.

The same principle is true in our spiritual lives. The slower and more thoughtfully we dine with God, the more value we receive from our encounter. *How* we spend our time in God's presence affects our relationship with him. It isn't enough just to show up and execute a discipline—to have a quiet time for the sake of fulfilling an obligation. That's a bit like eating too quickly, then wondering why you don't experience the nutritional benefits.

Women of a generous spirit look to Jesus for spiritual nourishment. Jesus said, "I am the bread of life. He who comes to me will never go hungry, and he who believes in me will never be thirsty" (John 6:35). He offers love, guidance, discernment, and the mystically spiritual power to live with amazing peace in the midst of great turmoil.

Even when pressed with time constraints and challenges, generous women do their best to spend time with God. It's not that they never skip a day or even a week, but when they do, it's as if they have not been in touch with their best friend. They rely on the strength their time with God gives them.

"I CAN'T GIVE WHEN I HAVEN'T TAKEN IN"

Several weeks after meeting Corky, I asked her how she managed to express such a loving spirit, given her very busy life. She has four children ranging in age from ten to twenty, owns a beautician business, volunteers one day a week as a hospital chaplain, and is involved in her church's women's ministry.

"I grew up in a giving family," she said. "There were seven kids and two bedrooms. The best we could do was to give ourselves and to share our gifts. My parents were very generous and modeled that constantly."

Corky went on to tell how God had healed her. "I am a wounded healer. Years ago my husband and I were sitting on top of the world. We were at the beginning of a great marriage and expecting our first child. I was four-and-a-half months pregnant and thanking God for everything. Then I had a miscarriage." Corky told me how devastated and confused she was. She questioned why God would let this happen to her. But as she spent time with him and told him how she felt, he began to comfort and heal her.

Corky continued, "A miracle occurred when I suddenly knew in my heart that I wanted his will, even when I didn't understand it. I knew I had to trust him. I knew, too, that he was trustworthy. Now I volunteer in the pediatric ward of the hospital. Just this week I was with parents whose infant is tremendously ill. After praying with them, I went back up to the nursery and prayed over their precious little one who won't be alive much longer."

I interrupted Corky as the painful memories of the day that my daughter miscarried brought fresh tears to my eyes. "How can you do that?" I asked her.

Corky talked about how grateful she was that God helped her through her own loss. She wants to make sure others know that God's love is available to them, so she gives in the same area where she experienced such pain. "I will never completely heal over my own loss, but Jesus fills me. I stay focused through prayer. I think of Mother Teresa's words about what she did when she felt overwhelmed. She looked at each person one at a time—she loved one person at a time. I trust God and his promises that he is with me, in me; I believe it because he gives me strength to do what he wants."

Corky stays filled by going to church every morning. "I knew that even serving could interfere with my spiritual growth," she said. "So I just decided to spend time each morning in quiet worship."

Through Corky I met Sandy, another woman who is "filled up" by her relationship with Jesus. "Every Monday, I have a desert day," Sandy said. "That's the day I stay at home and I pray and read Scripture . . . and do the laundry."

Sandy works full time as Director of Adult Ministries at her church, has raised six children, and has one granddaughter living with her now. I asked her how she managed to take one full day each week away from the busyness of life. "I've been doing it for about eight years and know I can't give to others when I don't. I turn on the answering machine, but now people seldom call on Monday. They know what I'm doing."

These two women can give without becoming bitter or burned out because they don't get depleted. They make sure they consistently receive the spiritual nourishment they need.

Paul, in his second letter to the Corinthians, said: "Now he who supplies seed to the sower and bread for food will also supply and increase your store of seed and will enlarge the harvest of your righteousness. You will be made rich in every way so that you can be generous on every occasion, and through us your generosity will result in thanksgiving to God" (2 Corinthians 9:10-11).

This verse says our relationship with God enables us to be *generous on every occasion*. I read the phrase *made rich in every way* and wonder if I really believe it. I know I probably define *every way* through my filter and need to adjust my thinking about what God really means. I also know that if I really believed that he will make me rich in every way—even ways I don't understand—I would be more motivated to be with him.

God gives us the strength and power to touch others with life-giving love. As we continually go to him, he meets our needs and fills us to overflowing. As he meets our needs, we are free to notice others' needs. Our time with God changes us from self-focused women into women who think about others.

At the end of my phone interview with Corky, I asked her if there was anything she wanted to add. She replied: "Just tell your daughter that a group of ladies out here in California will be praying for her baby due this summer."

Corky, Sandy, and other women of a generous spirit routinely practice spiritual exercises like daily time with God, prayer, and Bible reading. But they don't just go through the motions. They engage with him in ways that make significant differences in their lives.

An event that happened a few years ago highlighted for me that my own spiritual routines were just that—routine.

COMING TO THE TABLE

On March 16, 1993, the phone rang just as I was beginning to fix dinner. I know the exact date because I write down benchmark events on the margin of the chapter in Proverbs that corresponds to the date of the event.

On that day I wrote: *Craig tried to pitch—his arm wouldn't hold up.*

I read the words now and remember that wintry evening when my daughter's voice crackled over a poor phone connection between California and Colorado. "We're at the hospital," Lara said over the static. "Craig [her fiancé] was trying to pitch today, and his arm hurt so badly that he was taken out of the game, and we're here for him to have tests run."

Lara was a junior in college and was engaged to Craig, who is now her husband. Craig was also a junior at Point Loma Nazarene College and was a star pitcher on the baseball team. He had been recruited out of high school to play professional baseball but opted to go to college first. He anticipated a stellar future as he heard from a number of professional teams as his college years were drawing to a close.

"What do the tests show so far?" I asked Lara.

"We won't know for sure until Monday, but they think he may have a tumor."

Her words flooded my heart with fear.

Tumor.

"Well, call me as soon as you know anything at all." I sounded more calm than I felt.

"Okay, Mom," she replied, "and don't worry."

But anxious thoughts were already racing through my mind. Craig and Lara were so young, both had so much to look forward to. The thought of him having cancer paralyzed my soul, crowding out hope. I was sitting in a chair, crying, when Steve got home from work.

He tried to console me and remind me that the tests might not reveal a tumor at all. Still, I wallowed in fear. That night I prayed and cried and flailed before God with no relief.

The next day was no better, and I reluctantly went to an evening commitment with Steve. We were going to hear Richard Foster speak on spiritual disciplines. I didn't want to be subjected to a guilt trip about my lack of time spent in Bible reading and prayer. But Richard Foster surprised me. He spoke of spiritual disciplines in a way I had not considered before. Along with the familiar ones of Bible reading, prayer, study, and worship, he talked about the disciplines of meditation, fasting, simplicity, service, confession, and others. The illuminating moment for me was when he described the practice of spiritual disciplines as the means to position us to receive grace. I realized that grace was transforming and available, but I had not been in the right place to receive it.

His words reminded me of a wonderful man who had been active in evangelism training when I was still in Florida. Charlie led people to Christ in bountiful numbers. He wore a perpetual smile, which one day had caused me to ask someone what Charlie's life had been like. His friend told me of the many heartaches Charlie had lived through, including the brutal murder of his daughter when she was a young woman. I was shocked. Charlie was full of genuine joy and gifted at sharing that joy with others.

Another time someone in our class asked Charlie how he managed to stay so positive. He responded, "I stay under the spout where the blessings come out."

That night as I listened to Richard Foster, I pictured Charlie sitting in a chair with the blessings of God's grace pouring out on him and into his very soul. I understood, then, that Charlie received much from God because he was with him in an open way, listening, expressing, thinking. His heart and mind were focused on meeting with Jesus, not on performing some discipline because he had to.

I had to admit that my private time spent with God had become flat. I would sit in a chair and perfunctorily read the Bible, pray, close my Bible, and get on with my day. There was no heartfelt engagement. I didn't spend time listening or reflecting. I was just going through the motions. And therefore, I missed the benefit.

Foster writes about such empty externalism: "The Spiritual Disciplines are intended for our good. They are meant to bring the abundance of God into our lives. It is possible, however, to turn them into another set of soul-killing laws. Law-bound Disciplines breathe death."[1]

I had moved away from a grace-receiving position.

As we left the conference that night, my spirits were lifted. I couldn't wait to move spiritual disciplines back into my life and really meet with God, get to know him, and to receive all of what he has for me. My concern for Craig was still great, but it was no longer anxiety-ridden and paralyzing.

Three days later Lara called with good news. The suspected tumor was a bone spur. It did abruptly terminate Craig's baseball career, but his life was not in danger. I wept, this time with the tremendous relief of prayers answered as hoped for. I also told God that I had heard him; he could fill me if I would come to his table with a receptive heart, if I would interact with him.

It's easy to see that if we came to a dinner table with a damaged digestive system, the food we ate would be of no value. Imagine sitting down to a feast and stuffing delicious food into an internal tube that bypassed our stomachs and digestive systems. We would have eaten, but our bodies would receive no benefit.

The same is true if we meet with God and read his Word and pray but don't ingest his goodness. In order for God to be our *bread of life*, we must take time to develop the open, heart-engaged attitude of women who want to be in relationship with him. Through this relationship we receive real life and in turn have real life to give to others.

The buoyancy I experienced after hearing Richard Foster stayed with me for months. I discovered a growing heart connection between me and God that impacted my time with him. But after a while, it was increasingly easy to slip back to the old focus on externals. Habits stick to us like superglue.

Someone shared with me a writing exercise that has helped me keep my focus on God. This process has been especially helpful when I am upset. I have written in a journal for years and just inserted this exercise right into the pages of the journal. Whenever I am struggling with difficult circumstances and am trying to understand what God is saying or doing, I journal through these steps:

1. Meet with him: I go to a quiet place specifically to tell God my concerns.

2. Ask myself questions about what is bothering me: How do I feel? What am I fearful of? What do I think God thinks?

3. Write down my feelings: I write my honest, gut-level emotions in response to my own questions.

4. Reflect: Just sit quietly and think about sitting there with Jesus. I try to clear my mind of negative thoughts and to think about being with him and believing that he cares about my concerns.

5. Write down my thoughts: After a few minutes, I write down my thoughts.

6. Wait: I try just to sit in his presence. I try to focus on being with him. I end my time praying my honest feelings and my willingness to submit to his will.

7. Take one step of obedience: The time I have spent in this exercise might reveal to me a need for a specific action, so I determine to move in the direction of taking that action. The next step of obedience might be just to do whatever is next in the course of that day.

This process brings God actively into my life in a practical way. It allows me to get my hands on whatever is preventing me from receiving God's provision. And that is the key. It isn't enough to know that time with God brings fullness and power into our lives. We must absorb the spiritual mysteries of God's grace into our hearts in order to fill up on him.

FEEDING OTHERS

As we become women of a generous spirit, we will also relish relationships with women pursuing the same path. We will help each other absorb God's truth by talking, listening, encouraging, reflecting, and mulling over our thoughts together.

Our times alone with God may generate questions or birth fresh ideas that bubble up inside us. Discussions with other women can enhance our ability to discern what God is doing in our lives. As we talk with each other, our relationships with God are strengthened. But it doesn't stop there.

Our relationship with God is not meant to end with our meeting with him and receiving his love, acceptance, grace, and power. Nor are we to limit our friendships, to spend our time only with others who think as we do. We are also to give to those in need, both to those we know and those we don't.

Prior to his ascension, Jesus commanded his disciples to care for his sheep.

When they had finished eating, Jesus said to Simon Peter,
"Simon, son of John, do you truly love me more than these?"

"Yes, Lord," he said, "you know that I love you."

Jesus said, "Feed my lambs." Again Jesus said, "Simon,
son of John, do you truly love me?"

He answered, "Yes, Lord, you know that I love you."

Jesus said, "Take care of my sheep." The third time he
said to him, "Simon, son of John, do you love me?" Peter was
hurt because Jesus asked him the third time, "Do you love
me?"

He said, "Lord, you know all things; you know that I
love you."

Jesus said, "Feed my sheep." (John 21:15-17)

In this passage Jesus repeatedly asks Simon Peter to affirm his love for him. And with each affirmation, Jesus issues a command. Maybe the repetition highlights two realities: This is an important command, and even when we are filled to love overflowing, it will be difficult to accomplish.

When Jesus was asked what was the greatest commandment, he said: " 'Love the Lord your God with all your heart and with all your soul and with all your mind.' This is the first and greatest commandment. And the second is like it: 'Love your neighbor as yourself' " (Matthew 22:37).

These two passages highlight our primary response to receiving

the fullness of God. We are to love those within the family of believers ("my sheep") and love all others as well ("neighbors"). Like
Jesus, who came to serve, we are to give from our overflow.

❧

If you and I desire to become women of a generous spirit, we must
diligently pursue God, for the more we give to others, the more we
need to replenish our spirits.

"It is so basic," Elaine said. "I've heard all my life that I need to
read my Bible and pray. It has only been in the last few years that I
have really connected how I spend my time with the Lord to the
power in my own life to be giving. It's made a real difference."

"I'm no Martin Luther," Annie replied when asked about her
time spent with God. She was referring to Luther's practice of getting up earlier and earlier to spend time in prayer—the more he had
to do, the earlier he got up. "But I have learned not to cheat myself
out of my own nourishment. I need that time or I have no energy
at all," Annie continued.

With God, it is never too late to begin again.

Questions and Suggestions

1. Describe how you feel about your personal time with the
Lord, or your lack of it.

2. Write about your response to Richard Foster's premise that
the Spiritual Disciplines put us in a position to receive grace.

WOMEN OF A GENEROUS SPIRIT

3. Are you willing to try to integrate some of those disciplines into your life in order to get to know God better? Write your feelings about how that looks different from the ways you have practiced the disciplines before.

4. Schedule at least a short amount of time to sit alone with God this week . . . the week after . . . and so on.

5. Practice the exercise outlined in this chapter for more actively engaging with God on practical levels:

- Meet with him.
- Ask yourself questions about what is on your mind.
- Write down your feelings.
- Spend a few minutes reflecting on what you have written.
- Write down your thoughts.
- Wait, then pray.
- Take one step of obedience.

6. Pray that God will infuse your time with him with an awareness of authentic, powerful relationship.

7. Who are your spiritual peers—women with whom you can sit and talk freely about your relationship with God? If you don't have any such women in your life, pray and intentionally seek to develop those relationships.

8. Meet regularly with these friends and encourage each other in your journeys toward becoming generous spirits.

Chapter 7

Be Yourself

Shortly after Jack's death, a good friend of mine introduced me to the writings of Elisabeth Elliot. Elisabeth's first husband, Jim Elliot, and four other missionaries had been killed in 1956 in the Ecuadorian jungles by Auca Indians. I read *The Shadow of the Almighty*, Jim Elliot's biography, and greatly admired this young man who lost his life at the age of twenty-nine. But it was *The Savage My Kinsman* that captured my heart and inspired me in those early days of loss.

The Savage My Kinsman is the written and pictorial account of Elisabeth Elliot's year with the people who killed her husband. Elisabeth, Rachel Saint (sister of Nate Saint, one of the other slain missionaries), and Elisabeth's three-year-old daughter, Valerie, ventured into the remote jungles on a mission. They felt God's leading to go and bring the message of God's love to the Aucas and to translate the Scriptures into the Aucan language.

I leafed through the worn pages of *The Savage My Kinsman* for many nights and lingered over the photographs that depicted remarkable sacrifice and courage. I still remember several: one of Elisabeth with her head bowed as she prayed by candlelight about her future; another of Elisabeth settled in her grass hut, reading in a mesh hammock; and the last photograph in the book capturing her daughter, just a young child, walking hand in hand with one of the men who killed her father.

After my own daughters were tucked safely in for the night, I would crawl into my own bed and ponder the remarkable faith of Elisabeth Elliot. A measure of God's healing touch in my life-adjusting-to-loss was accomplished through the visual testimony of this woman. *If she could do THAT,* I would say to myself, *then I can certainly honor God with my life.*

While I never took steps to become a missionary, I viewed missions as the ideal of a giving spirit, the ultimate way to serve God. Questions arose whenever I pictured Elisabeth Elliot in that jungle and me in my comfortable home: Should I go far away in order to serve God? Did generous giving mean leaving family? Did sacrifice mean giving up material comfort?

The questions lingered until three years later, when something happened that finally put them to rest. I had decided to move from Florida to Colorado. The moving van came one day, and we left the next morning, stuffed into our station wagon for the drive across the country. A woman, two girls, and a basset-hound puppy headed west on a pioneer adventure.

As expected, we arrived ahead of the moving van and spent our first night at a motel. The girls convinced me we should spend the second night in the house, even if the moving van hadn't arrived. I agreed, and we set up makeshift beds on the floor of the empty living room.

In the middle of the night, I was awakened by a strange sound. I abruptly sat up and listened to a hurried rustling coming from the kitchen. Jumping up from my bed on the floor, I went into the dining room and hit the light switch just in time to see a mouse scurry out of the dog-food bag leaning against the kitchen wall.

My screams jarred the girls and the puppy out of their sound sleep. The mouse was out of sight, probably quaking at the alarming chaos unfolding around him. I was hopping in a kind of stutter step, attempting to shake off the hundreds of phantom mice I felt crawling up my legs.

Admittedly, I have mouse-a-phobia. While I learned in Florida to squash a cockroach with my bare fist, I have never overcome my fear of those tiny, furry creatures. Since we had no furniture in the house, there was no place to get psychologically out-of-reach from our intruder.

There was no way I would lie back down on the floor. I started shouting to Lisa and Lara to gather up some clothes and head to the car. I grabbed my bathrobe and car keys and began nudging our confused basset hound toward the door.

"Where are we going, Mom?" Lisa asked.

"I don't know," I replied. "Just get out of the house."

Once in the car, I began to relax. We would go to a motel for the rest of the night and call an exterminator in the morning. Once the grim reaper for four-legged varmints had cleared the house, we would return.

I pulled up to the office of a nearby motel and charged toward the front desk. The night clerk raised an eyebrow at the sight of a harried woman in a bathrobe running into the motel at 3:00 A.M.

"Is something wrong?" he asked.

"Oh, you bet," I replied.

I launched into a lengthy explanation of why we were moving from our house and into a motel in the middle of the night. The clerk looked suspiciously back at me and expressed no sympathy or understanding of our plight.

"It's half-price," was his only remark.

"What is?" I asked, surprised at his disinterest in my story.

"The room rate—it's half-price if you arrive after midnight," he flatly replied.

"Oh, great!" I said, my spirits beginning to lift.

As I lay safely in the motel bed, I thought about the many nights I had looked at the pictures of Elisabeth Elliot in the jungles of Ecuador, romanticizing her work and comparing mine to hers.

Obviously—and for good reason—God had not called me to the mission field. He could use me in other ways.

Elisabeth Elliott writes: "According to expectation, when the time came to do something, the guidance was unmistakable."[1] I had not received unmistakable guidance about mission work. I had only looked at God working in one woman and assumed that what she did was the ideal.

FOLLOWING GOD'S UNIQUE DESIGN

I thought being a missionary was the ideal way to serve God. I had neglected to consider my own uniqueness. God doesn't ask us to serve in the same way as others. If we see ourselves only as inadequate reflections of someone else, we may give up our pursuit of becoming life-givers. We see our attempts to give as failures when compared to the successes of others. But instead of being threatened by visibly giving women, let's learn from them while we become the women God made us to be.

We can be ourselves—we can be authentic—and serve God where we are. When we live in authenticity, we don't try to be someone other than who we are. We don't seek to impress people or to live up to their expectations for our lives. We go to God for discernment about how our unique gifts are to be expressed.

When we don't give in ways consistent with who we are, people often sense it and may question our motives. *Why is she being so giving in this way? What does she want?* Haven't we all experienced duplicity and wondered what really lies beneath the surface?

"I had a friend who used to do very giving things for me," Toni told me. "But I always felt like she was gritting her teeth, like she didn't really want to watch my kids or bring over a meal. I felt like she was doing what she thought she should, but it wasn't really her."

Toni's friend probably meant well, but she may have been acting out of obligation instead of her individual uniqueness. She may not have moved from the bondage of trying to live up to some ideal to the freedom of recognizing the ideal in herself.

When we are free to be who God made us to be, we no longer feel obligated to say yes simply because that's what others expect or because there is a need. We won't feel guilty that we have let someone down.

When I asked her about ways of giving that don't reflect who she is personally, Jan told me, "I don't like making meals for people. I don't like to cook, and I'm not that good at it." Jan's honesty comes from her desire to give out of fullness instead of guilt or an idealized image of what generous women ought to be doing.

While in an emergency Jan is certainly willing to do things she is uncomfortable with, she enjoys the freedom to decline to give in ways that don't reflect her strengths. Instead she offers to give in ways that do. Jan understands the wisdom expressed in this African proverb: "A frog tried to look as big as the elephant and burst."

When we try to be something other than who God made us to be, it doesn't work—at least for long.

ENJOYING OUR FREEDOM

I had a front-row seat in observing just how great it feels when we gain the freedom to be ourselves. I had always assumed both my daughters were extroverts. They easily converse, laugh, meet strangers, and enjoy being around other people. Their father was an extrovert, and I am an off-the-scale one. After Jack died, a good friend of mine, Susan, moved in with us for a while. Susan, too, is an extrovert.

Susan joined Lisa, Lara, and me one year on summer vacation. I had taken along a book about personalities that included a test to determine your personality type. We all took the test, and, much to my surprise, Lisa's answer revealed that she is an introvert. She wasn't surprised, however, and expressed great relief to read a description of the normal feelings of an introvert.

Lisa gained her freedom that day. Each of us read about the way introverts feel and relate and changed our perceptions about her. Lisa enjoys being behind the scenes and was relieved not to be singled out to tell a story or explain her feelings. She has exceptional ability with detailed planning and has eased my schedule by handling my radio and speaking bookings. Talking in front of a group is not her idea of a good time, but she gives from her own unique strength when she arranges the logistics that enable me to speak to people across the country.

Women of a generous spirit give in ways consistent with their uniqueness. They don't look at other women and copy their actions. While they may learn from others and incorporate some of their expressions of giving, women of a generous spirit have learned who they are. They, like Lisa, have discovered that their personalities play a part in how they give. They experience freedom in expressing who they are, and they release others to be who they are.

FREEING OTHERS TO BE THEMSELVES

Generous spirits also applaud other women in their personal successes. When they do, they free others to be themselves. I learned this by default.

I used to love kamikaze evangelism: hitting the streets and knocking on the doors of strangers, asking them questions about their spiritual beliefs. At the time, I was attending a church that expected everyone to participate in evangelism training. Every member was encouraged to get involved and stay involved. Because of my own enthusiasm, I couldn't understand why everyone didn't WANT to go out into the highways and byways and lasso the unsuspecting.

A good friend of mine, Nancy, didn't share my viewpoint. Although she was quiet and shy, she was the wife of one of the associate pastors and, therefore, required to be trained in evangelism. Week after week Nancy agonized through the grueling task of going out and talking to strangers. Her discomfort and disappointment drained her energies and robbed her of joy in the areas where she truly loved to give.

Years later Nancy moved away and became involved in a church in ways that more consistently reflected her own uniqueness. She is a gifted musician and gracious hostess. Her hospitality and warm, inviting spirit provide a safe place for many to rest and regroup. She is an encourager and faithful friend.

When I saw the change in her, I realized that I had been among the enthusiastic evangelists who imposed my gifts and strengths on others, including her. I was sorry for my own arrogant attitudes about how every person in the body of Christ should serve. We are all called to testify to the reality of Jesus in our lives, but we are not all called to witness in the same way. I can now appreciate and praise Nancy's gifts of music and hospitality without thinking she should also be out knocking on doors evangelizing. I can also accept that I have no musical talent, and that's okay.

Often, applauding others' successes means laying down any competitive attitudes we may have. We all want to be first, to be noticed, to receive the loudest applause. It isn't godly to have these attitudes, but they reside in all of us. Yet if we desire to be life-giving women, we will assume a position beside each other, not opposite. We are on the same team, but we don't all play the same position.

Each of us fulfills one role, and we help others fulfill their roles. The late tennis professional Arthur Ashe said, "True heroism is remarkably sober, very undramatic. It is not the urge to surpass all others at whatever cost, but the urge to serve others at whatever cost."

One way of serving does not outrank any other way of serving. Paul reminds us to free others to be who they are without any arrogance on our part: "For by the grace given me I say to every one of you: Do not think of yourself more highly than you ought, but rather think of yourself with sober judgment, in accordance with the measure of faith God has given you. Just as each of us has one body with many members, and these members do not all have the same function, so in Christ we who are many form one body, and each member belongs to all the others" (Romans 12:3-5).

WHAT GOD WANTS FOR US

The one we follow calls us just to be who he made us to be.

The other day I asked Justin what he wants to be when he grows up. "Justin," he replied.

"I know you're Justin," I said, trying to explain, "but Nana wants to know what you want to be."

"Justin, just Justin," he said emphatically.

He understands so much better than I do, I thought.

Just me, just as God means for me to be; just you, just as God means for you to be. That's what God wants.

Questions and Suggestions

1. Write down three words that you think your friends would use to describe you.

2. Write down three words that you would use to describe yourself—be honest, no one else needs to see this.

3. Think about how similar your public persona is to who you feel you really are.

4. What facades do you need to abandon to be free to give from who you are?

5. Who are the people you hold in judgment because you find them lacking in the ways that they give?

6. Who are the people you hold in judgment because you have a spirit of envy or comparison toward them?

7. Pray, and continue praying, for God to enable you to release all of them from your judgment.

Chapter 8

Helping Others Encounter God

In the movie *Michael,* John Travolta plays a wayward angel traveling across the country from the Midwest to New York. While this movie couldn't be endorsed as presenting a godly representation of angels, it does provide an interesting illustration: While standing in the middle of a group of people, Michael predicts what one young woman will do next.

Another woman standing by him asks how he knew that. Expecting him to profess something about his spiritual powers, the audience is surprised to hear him say, "I pay attention."

What a great line! *I pay attention.*

Often we don't pay attention. But the more we do, the more likely we will touch others in significant ways. We need to pay attention. If we don't, we're apt to make assumptions that simply aren't true.

In this chapter we'll look at ways to be life-givers to those who don't know God. To do this effectively, we need to pay attention . . . we need to pay attention to how we are being perceived by those who do not believe as we do.

Our country no longer accepts Judeo-Christian values as the norm. The gap is widening between the values of those who follow Jesus and the values of those who don't. The actions and words of Christians are highlighted on the evening news and discussed on talk shows. No longer hidden under a bushel, Christians are being identified and quoted and evaluated.

Even if we are not personally involved in public debates . . . even if we are not the Christians featured on the evening news, because we claim the name of Christ, we are often identified with those who are. In many circles, Christians are being labeled as a group that cares more that society adopt their values than for the individuals in that society. Many who don't know Jesus are suspicious of Christians because they perceive us to be judgmental and arrogant.

I will never forget the meeting in which this was brought home for me.

UNDERSTANDING THE WAY WE ARE PERCEIVED

Steve and I sat on the floor against the wall of the jam-packed auditorium of Colorado College. It was early in 1993, just months after Amendment Two was passed and added to the Colorado Constitution. The amendment was "the nation's first statewide ban on laws specifically aimed at protecting gays from discrimination based on sexual orientation."[1] It has since been declared unconstitutional, but it was one of the key inflammatory ingredients in our community's response to Christians' involvement in public life.

The college auditorium was filled with visibly agitated citizens fearful of the power of the Christian community credited with politicking the amendment into law. At the time Steve was the religion editor for the city newspaper, the *Gazette Telegraph*, but he wasn't officially covering this event. We had come because we were concerned about the growing polarization between the secular and Christian communities in Colorado Springs since the amendment had passed.

I couldn't believe the energy sweeping through the room; people lined the walls and aisles, and voices rose as the intensity of conversations escalated. I felt as if Steve and I had slipped into a scene in a novel designed to create a salient tension between good and evil. In this case, the guys in the white hats were the average citizens of the city, and the guys in the black hats were the Christians who had infiltrated a peaceful community and turned it upside down with their political power.

The meeting was sponsored by Citizen's Project, an organization formed the year before to watchdog the political activity of the Christian community in Colorado Springs. This city of 450,000 has over fifty parachurch organizations and some four hundred churches. Their statewide political impact had alarmed the general public. Public school educators and parents were in dispute with Christians over school curriculum. One church had baptized children it bussed in for vacation Bible school without their parents' permission. Then Amendment Two passed.

After a brief presentation, the floor was opened for questions. For the next hour I sat and listened to people voice their concerns about Christians. Some went so far as to compare the beginnings of the Nazi movement and Hitler's prejudice against non-Aryans to Christians and their prejudice against homosexuals. Others quoted Christian battle rhetoric they had heard or read and were worried about its meaning. Many puzzled over the hateful attitude they perceived to be a mandatory requirement of being a Christian.

One lone man stood and calmly observed that all Christians were not as this group feared. He implored the audience not to be so fearful and to understand that there was a lot of misunderstanding between the two groups. But despite this man's gentle and loving spirit, his words were jeered from the audience while the founder of Citizen's Project tried to encourage respect for this solitary voice.

I sat on the sidelines in shock. These unbelievers feared Christians! They didn't know us by our love. They thought we hated them. They had even compared Christians to Hitler! What had happened? How had Christians come to be so identified with hate instead of with Jesus, who came to earth to die for us? Where was the association of Christians with a just but loving God? These people knew exactly how Christians felt about a number of political issues, but they did not know about the grace of the gospel! How could we possibly gain a platform to tell them the good news in ways they could hear?

I cried all the way home. It wasn't the first time I'd heard how the secular community viewed Christians, but it was the first time that the intensity of their feelings and the distance between believer and nonbeliever had been so vividly played out in front of me.

In the midst of such passionate debates, even loving and caring words can be ignored or misunderstood. Sadly, when Christians *do* try to love those with whom they disagree, it's often not received because of the assumption that all Christians are judgmental.

If we want to be life-giving women, we will pay attention to this. We will also be wise in how we communicate our passionate concerns and deep desires to be part of positive change in the lives of unbelievers. I can't think of a better example than Jesus on how to do this.

TREATING SINNERS AS JESUS DID

The teachers of the law and the Pharisees brought in a woman caught in adultery. They made her stand before the group and said to Jesus, "Teacher, this woman was caught in the act of adultery. In the Law Moses commanded us to stone such women. Now what do you say?" They were using this question as a trap, in order to have a basis for accusing him.

But Jesus bent down and started to write on the ground with his finger. When they kept on questioning him, he straightened up and said to them, "If any one of you is without sin, let him be the first to throw a stone at her." Again he stooped down and wrote on the ground.

At this, those who heard began to go away one at a time, the older ones first, until only Jesus was left, with the woman still standing there. Jesus straightened up and asked her, "Woman, where are they? Has no one condemned you?"

"No one, sir," she said.

"Then, neither do I condemn you," Jesus declared. "Go now and leave your life of sin." (John 8:3-11)

The teachers of the law and the Pharisees wanted to trick Jesus, so they used the woman caught in adultery as a pawn to further their agenda. Roman law did not allow Jews to carry out the death sentence, but Jewish law commanded stoning for adulterous women. The Pharisees tried to put Jesus in a double bind: If he had said not to stone her, he would have been breaking Moses' law, but if he had said to stone her, they could have reported him to the Roman authorities for breaking Roman law.

So what did Jesus do? He responded by bending down and writing on the ground. He told the woman's accusers to look back at themselves and their own sins. At this, the attempts to manipulate Jesus ceased, and the apparent conviction of their own sin drove the teachers and Pharisees away.

The Pharisees were not concerned about the woman they brought to Jesus. Had Jesus not intervened, her exposure as an adulteress would probably have led to her death. They gave no thought to how they might give her life, let alone spiritual life. Their focus was to trap Jesus—they had their own agenda. (Sound familiar?)

But something happened when they encountered Jesus face to face. They didn't argue or defend themselves, nor did they accuse him of being hateful or arrogant. His words had the power to send them away quietly. The adulterous woman also found herself face to face with Jesus. We don't know what he wrote on the ground, and we don't know what she did after she left Jesus. But we do know how he treated her. We know he didn't condemn her—nor did he ignore her sin.

The Bible tells us to speak "the truth in love" (Ephesians 4:15). This is what Jesus did. He bent down and had a private exchange with the woman. He took the heat off of her by pointing her accusers toward their own sin. He did not condemn her, and after she had the opportunity to really encounter him, he told her to leave her life of sin. His actions and his words were life-giving.

All of us who have a personal relationship with Christ have been in the position of both the woman and her accusers. We have been pardoned and commanded to turn from our sins. We have also read and studied the words of Scripture and determined principles about how we should live. We have embraced those principles and try to live by them.

But when we meet nonbelievers, how do we respond? Are we like Jesus? Do our hearts break over their God-less lives? Or do we see their sin and want to bring them to justice? Does an encounter with us help those who don't know Jesus to come closer to an encounter with him?

Like Jesus, women of a generous spirit consider their attitudes toward non-Christians. They don't judge them from afar while offering no opportunity for relationship. Two women I know have shown me better how to do this.

Marty hosts quarterly teas at her home and invites all the women on her block. She doesn't have any specific agenda except to get to know these women. Many of her neighbors are not Christians but have noticed the spirit of friendship that Marty extends. They have responded to her invitations with gratitude, and some have started to call her to talk about their lives. Marty is able, by listening and being patient, to communicate God's love to them in non-judgmental ways. God's love is her focus, without ignoring sin.

Janice lived in the same apartment building with Ilene. Janice had invited Ilene to come to church with her, but she had refused. One day they bumped into each other in the laundry room, and Ilene tearfully told Janice that she was pregnant and unmarried. Janice suggested they meet for lunch the next day. During the next few months, Janice befriended Ilene by meeting with her, listening to her, and responding with kindness. Eventually Ilene was open to God's love through a relationship with Jesus and began attending church with Janice. Several other women became involved and provided the support that Ilene needed to begin her life as a single mother.

These women didn't condone Ilene's behavior that led to her pregnancy, but they showed her love and acceptance that led to Ilene's life-changing encounter with God.

For Jesus' sake, it matters HOW we talk about our faith in Christ and the values which are founded in that faith. The results are up to God, but we are not absolved of our responsibility to consider the response of our audience. It is up to us to invite those who differ with us to come into our lives. Are we drawing them closer to an encounter with God or are we part of what might be preventing such an encounter?

CLEARING THE PATH

Maybe you are reading this and thinking, *I have never communicated judgment about others or spoken in a public meeting, so what does this have to do with me?*

We need to realize that the way any individual Christian or Christian organization communicates represents all of us. And because of today's sophisticated technology a small incident in one part of the world becomes news in all corners of the world. We may be talking over coffee with a woman in our hometown who has formed an opinion about God and Christians because of something she read on the Internet that morning.

Even when we are wronged, we are to respond with the love of Christ operative in our lives. People who do not know him are not under that obligation. That does not mean that we are to be doormats in our society, but we are to take our firm stands with humility, graciousness, and the evidence of hearts broken over people not knowing the love of God.

Christianity Today published an article by Michael Hamilton that related how many years ago Francis Schaeffer struggled with his own strong convictions and the lack of Christian love he saw from many believers:

> *In the end, he found a new assurance that his doctrine was correct and that the "real battle for men is in the world of ideas," but also a new conviction that orthodox belief must travel hand in hand with demonstrative love. "The local church or Christian group should be right, but it should also be beautiful. The local group should be the example of the supernatural, of the substantially healed relationship in this present life between men and men. . . . How many orthodox local churches are dead at this point, with so little sign of love and communication: orthodox, but dead and ugly! If there is*

no reality on the local level, we deny what we say we
believe."²

Unless offered in love, our giving will be ill-received and our professions of our beliefs suspect. We can't say we love people and then act in ways that communicate condemnation. If we do, our agendas, like those of the teachers of the law and the Pharisees, will rule over our concern that people encounter Jesus.

If we want to be women of a generous spirit, we'll hold unswervingly to our beliefs while removing obstacles that impede the way to Jesus. We'll risk involvement with the people whose conflicting voices may cause us to want to run to the cloister of the Christian ghetto. Like Jesus, we won't remain in safe places.

MOVING OUT OF OUR COMFORT ZONES

For some, that may mean doing something unfamiliar, something out of our comfort zones. Ann has dinner once a month with a group of believers and nonbelievers who get together to discuss issues of common interest in the community. The organization sponsoring these meetings and others like it is called Food for Thought. A facilitator helps the participants remain respectful and communicate without hostility.

"I got involved because I realized that I didn't understand why so many people viewed Christians as unloving," Ann said. "It has been an eye-opening experience. I had no idea that so many mis-conceptions are floating around about why Christians act the way they do. We are seen as arrogant and judgmental, and these people can quote things they have heard believers say that make them feel that way.

"The other people in our group are a mix—an atheist, a Jewish man, a former Lutheran, an agnostic, and another Christian couple besides my husband and me. Our discussions are lively, to say the least.

"I guess the thing that strikes me the most is how complicated the whole issue is of why people believe what they believe. These people are nice, caring people with good marriages, who care about their children. But they think very differently than I do as a Christ-ian. Sometimes it takes a very long time to say anything about my faith because we spend so much time dealing with particular issues that only reflect beliefs. Talking about why the beliefs are there comes later."

Ann admitted that she has considered dropping out because the dinners are time-consuming and sometimes seem fruitless. "But," she said, "I stay in because I really do want to bring Jesus into the sphere of these people's lives. They see Christians in such a negative light, and they don't see Jesus at all."

Margaret, another woman involved in Food for Thought, ex-pressed her frustration at the hesitancy of many Christians even to give the dinners a try. "We have gone to a number of churches to present the opportunity to meet nonbelievers in a friendly setting, but we've had little positive response. One woman told me she just couldn't be around all those feminists and not get mad. I felt awful that she leveled such a judgment without even considering meeting any of the people involved."

Margaret went on to say she understood that many people are fearful of engaging so directly with nonbelievers. It is scary to think about being put on the spot to answer about our beliefs.

START RIGHT WHERE YOU ARE

You may be reading this and thinking the same thing. There may be no structured group in your area to help you facilitate this kind of dinner. But you could try something on a smaller scale: Simply get to know people outside your church or the Christian community. Be yourself and allow them to be themselves. Lay down the goal of making every contact with non-Christians a time when you *must* tell them the plan of salvation and pick up the one of getting to know your neighbors—or the parents of your children's classmates, or the woman you talk to each week at the aerobics class. That's all. Get to know them and pray for them. Show hospitality, be gracious, talk about their interests, and share some of yours. See what happens. Take the time to build relationships and allow God to open doors for conversation to eventually get around to spirituality. Then your words about God's wonderful gift of his Son will carry power.

If we truly want to touch others with life-giving love, we'll make some tough choices. We may have to give up a night at home each week or once a month. We may have to make an effort to get to know the neighbors we've lived next to for the last ten years. It is certainly easier just to ask them to come to church than it is to actually get to know them. If they turn down our offer to come to church, then we can soothe our consciences by thinking we did all we could do.

Women of a generous spirit get involved with people who do not know Jesus because they love their Lord. He is worth it. And he has asked us to tell others about him. We are to follow him and live in ways that bring others into encounters with him. He is worth our efforts to understand, pay attention, and give generously from the fullness of his love.

Questions and Suggestions

1. Write down your honest feelings about non-Christians with whom you have strong disagreements. These people do not need to be people you know personally.

2. Write a paragraph about how you think you are perceived by non-Christians.

3. Do you see anything in your communication that might be an obstacle to a nonbeliever encountering Jesus? What and how?

4. What are some ways you can become a better listener?

5. Who are the non-Christians with whom you have somewhat regular contact? If there are none, pray about change.

6. Invite some non-Christians over for dinner—a fun evening, just social and caring.

Chapter 9

We Can't Do Everything

I unlocked the safety gate around the nursing home. Several patients greeted me with smiles and waves as they enjoyed the early briskness of fall in Colorado. One patient in particular, a woman in her early forties, had endeared herself to me. Amy suffered from severe mental confusion, rendering her totally disoriented at times and engagingly chatty at others. Confidentiality did not permit the staff to divulge the specifics of Amy's condition, so I just related to her as best I could on any given day.

Amy loved clothes and often changed outfits several times during my visits with my father. She would come and find me and show me her latest fashion concoction. I would make a fuss over her choices, and she'd be off to change again.

On this particular day, I had brought several sweat suits for Amy that my daughters no longer needed. I saw her strolling in the hallway just outside my father's room and went up to her with arms outstretched. She folded into my hug with excited talk about how glad she was to see me.

"I brought you something, Amy." I held out the bag the clothes were in.

"What is it?" she asked as she peered over the edge. "Oh boy! It's clothes!"

She started yanking the clothes out as I attempted to keep them from cascading all over the hall. "Why don't we go to your room, Amy, and I'll put your name on these and put them away for you?"

A passing nurse overheard me and offered to get a marker to label the clothes. Amy and I walked arm in arm to her room as she thanked me again and again. I laid the bag of clothes on the bed and began to take them out for the second time in a few minutes. My intent was to mark them and put them away for Amy, but she had other ideas.

She started to undress rather frantically, ignoring my entreaties for her to wait until the nurse returned with the marker. Her demeanor had shifted from excited to annoyed. She tugged at her sweater and mumbled in frustration because the snugness of the neckline was messing up her hair.

I didn't want to leave her but felt helpless about how to slow down her growing agitation. She didn't even seem aware that I was still in the room. I handed her a sweatshirt only to have her rip off her remaining clothes and streak past me.

She ran naked out into the hall with arms waving and voice escalating. I collapsed in a chair in her room, knowing the staff would intercept her and bring her safely back. As her yells grew fainter, I dropped my head in my hands and began to cry. I had not meant to upset Amy. She loved clothes, and I thought I would make her happy by bringing her some.

As I listened to the distant sound of scurrying feet and calming voices, I realized how limited I was to offer significant help to any of the patients who resided with my father. Their needs and my father's needs were well beyond my understanding. These mentally wounded men and women required competent people to keep them from harm and to bring them joy. I felt useless.

I slowly walked back to my father's room. As I sat and visited with him, Amy ran past the door several times with nurses close behind her trying to catch her. The other patients didn't even seem to notice a disruption in their own veiled worlds.

Finally Amy was cut off at a corner and rescued by two nurses. They very sweetly took her by each arm and started to walk her back to her room. Their words and gentle, firm touch immediately calmed her. She willingly relaxed between these two caregivers, and the trauma of the moment was over.

As I was leaving, I stopped by the nurses' station and apologized for upsetting Amy.

"I only meant to help," I offered weakly. "I'm so sorry."

The nurse behind the counter smiled warmly and assured me

that nothing damaging had occurred. She thanked me for the clothes for Amy and said that my visits with Amy were a bright spot in her troubled life.

Recognizing our limitations is humbling. When faced with our inadequacies in helping others, we often feel incompetent. We feel as if we should be able to do more. While I was frustrated about my inability to comfort Amy, I felt much worse about not being able to help my father. All I could do was visit him, knowing he would forget I was there the minute I left his room. The staff continued to tell me that my visits were meaningful, and they thanked me profusely for my part in my father's care. Jesus said, "My yoke is easy and my burden is light" (Matthew 11:30). Perhaps the yoke he intends for us to carry looks different than the one we presume he places on us. Perhaps he means for us to do less than we imagine. Perhaps our "less" can still have significant impact.

GIVING EVEN A LITTLE HELPS

When I wrote *Daughters without Dads,* I interviewed several psychologists about the impact of absent fathers in the lives of women. Sometimes the fathers had died, but often they were absent because of a divorce. Several psychologists told me that many fathers who are not the primary custodial parent think that giving in little ways is not valuable for their daughters. These men often quit visiting or acknowledging birthdays and other special events because they feel guilty about being part-time fathers. They miss the positives in their daughters' lives that even small touches from them can bring.

"My father used to call me on holidays and send letters a few times a year," Bonnie said. "I tried to tell him how much it meant to me for him to do that, but I don't think he heard me. I haven't heard from him now in over three years. I guess he has completely forgotten about me."

Bonnie was in her midthirties when she expressed her sadness over lack of contact with her father. The calls and few letters a year mattered to her.

Sometimes we can give only a little, but maybe we can give a little in generous ways and still touch others. We can take a moment and write that note we've meant to write for weeks. We can stop and pray for someone's hurts that have been brought to our attention. We can allow our hearts to be touched by needs that we cannot meet.

A friend of mine told me that every time she passes an automobile accident she prays for the people involved. She doesn't stop if someone else has arrived on the scene, but she prays for the strangers going through tough situations. They never know she prayed, but she hopes her prayers make a difference in their lives anyway.

All of us can think of people who have significantly touched us, even if only briefly.

Every Friday afternoon of my junior year in high school, my English teacher, Catherine Bryson, would read aloud for the last fifteen minutes of class. Any passerby might have been perplexed to see an advanced English class engaged in an activity usually associated with pre-readers. Miss Bryson's love of literature inspired her to interrupt our traditional education by bringing written words to life with her voice.

In my senior year, my adventure with words was enhanced by another dedicated teacher. Amy J. Wocko required weekly writing assignments which incorporated everything we had studied that week. Her attention to detail proved maddening to me, and every Friday I was ready just to slide into the weekend. But that was when we did in-class writing, pushing our discipline right up to the wire.

Miss Wocko's critique and her praise were as detailed as her requirements. She rewarded our efforts and communicated genuine concern for our growth as writers.

I haven't seen either of these women for over thirty years, but they created significant ripples that have had far-reaching effects. My love of words and confidence to dare to write began with Miss Bryson and Miss Wocko.

When I am discouraged about the overwhelming needs around me and my limitations in meeting them, I remind myself of the touch so many people have had in my own life. Like my high school English teachers, many loving people have dropped a pebble of wisdom, a kind word, an encouraging note into my life that helped to meet my needs. You and I may never know the difference our contributions have made.

VALUE VARYING DEGREES OF GIVING

I've become more comfortable with my limited ability to help others as I've realized that our giving flows out from us like water spraying out from a fountain. The pressure and density of the water is greater near the fountain's spout. As the water gurgles up and spills over, it is transformed from a surging gush into sprinkling droplets that splatter far and wide.

The same is true with the intensity of our giving. We cannot give equally to everyone. We give in proportion to the level of relationship we experience. Those that are closest to us receive the most intense generosity. Those further out still are replenished by our touch, but not in the same degree.

It would be impossible to give to everyone in the same way, but we can still be generous spirits. Like the fountain's sprinkling droplets, our generous giving falls on some lightly, bringing life in a measure that is combined with the giving of others.

When my friend prays for the people she passes who are in automobile accidents, she is part of a concert of giving. There are the people who arrive on the scene, the doctors, the families of the victims, their friends. My friend's contribution is not equal to the involvement of others, but her generous spirit carries prayers to heaven on behalf of hurting people. The answers to those prayers sprinkle down on people she doesn't even know.

TAKING CARE OF OURSELVES

We not only are limited in what we can do for others, but we also often limit what we can do for ourselves by neglecting the recreational side of our lives. A friend of mine was asked recently what she did for fun. "I actually couldn't think of anything specific," Marie told me. "I don't know if it's because I feel guilty or am just busy and don't schedule things for myself, but I just don't."

We all need the refreshment that lighthearted play or restful relaxation gives us. We know that God rested and we are to follow his example. But we don't.

Sundays were days of rest and fun when I was growing up. Even though I wasn't reared in a religious home, my family was part of the greater culture that took Sunday off. Stores were closed, chores around the house were untouched, the whole pace of life slowed to a refreshing calm. We used to go for Sunday drives or have picnics or enjoy playing board games.

Today the pace on Sunday does not always reflect the rejuvenating break that was the norm years ago. We don't routinely take a day to relax. Sometimes we go for weeks at a time without taking time for fun.

We don't need to take a day every week to be restored, but we may need to think about what relaxes us, makes us laugh, and relieves the tension of living at breakneck speed most of the time.

"I am renewed when I go with a friend to Old Colorado City," Jan said, "and walk, talk, eat lunch at a fun restaurant, and just relax."

"I love to just be with my husband and children," Cindy answered when I asked her how she recharges her batteries. "Even if we just go for a ride, it renews me."

Women of a generous spirit nurture the child within them. They know what revitalizes them, and they don't feel guilty for engaging in healthy play. They recognize the need for relationships with peers that infuse their lives with laughter and mutual encouragement.

Trudy and Cathy have begun to plug fun evenings into their friendship. Both love movies and talking for hours over coffee in the morning, and Cathy loves to cook. So every other Friday night, they meet at Cathy's house for dinner and a video. Trudy spends the night, and they linger over coffee on Saturday morning before she heads home. These intentional evenings flavor their lives with seemingly frivolous breaks that deeply feed their spirits.

I love to punctuate my busy schedule with a stop at a bookstore/coffee shop downtown. The main, book-lined room, furnished with comfortable tables and chairs, is next to the coffee shop with its pots of brewing coffee. I claim a favorite seat by the window and sit with my coffee-of-the-day. Then I write or read and sip the steaming coffee. Sometimes I only have an hour to linger in the pleasant ambiance of this quiet place, but that's enough to invigorate me.

Fun comes in many forms and can breathe new life into weary spirits. We routinely need to sprinkle a little into our lives. When we do, we are in many ways expressing our faith and confidence in our sovereign God. It is not up to us to fix the world!

RESTING IN CONFIDENCE

Be encouraged: Our limitations to help others don't limit God. We can rest in confidence that we don't have to do it all—God is at work. A recent event gave me a wonderful picture of what it means to rest in confidence.

"Please pray for Beau," Loretta said to me over the phone. Beau is the canine member of Loretta's family. She, her husband, and three children live in suburban Colorado Springs, and that provides Beau with lots of open space in which to roam.

"What's wrong with Beau?" I asked.

"Well, we came home this afternoon, and Beau had been with us. We got out of the van and left the garage door up. At dinnertime the kids called Beau, but he didn't come in. We haven't seen him since this afternoon, so I'm going to ride around the neighborhood and call for him."

"I'll be praying," I promised.

A few minutes later the phone rang again.

Loretta was laughing as I picked up the receiver.

"Lois, you won't believe where Beau was," she began.

"Where?"

"I opened the door of the van, and he was sitting shotgun," Loretta said with a smile in her voice.

The dog had never gotten out of the van when Loretta and her kids returned home. They had shut the doors, unaware that Beau was still inside. Loretta described how he just yawned and stretched his way out of the car some six hours after being locked in.

What a picture of resting in confidence! That dog knew his family would come back for him. He didn't know what they were doing, but he obviously wasn't concerned about his own situation or theirs.

Can't we do the same?

Questions and Suggestions

1. Write down needs you now see that cause you to feel overwhelmed.

2. Are there some people in your life who expect you to do more for them than you are able to do or more than you should do?

3. Pray about when and how to communicate to them that you are a limited resource. Lovingly express to them that you are setting some limits.

4. What do you do in your life for fun?

5. Put some fun things on your calendar, and don't let them get pushed off.

6. When unnecessary worry for others creeps into your thinking, practice resting in confidence that God is at work in their lives.

Chapter 10

The Ebb and Flow of Giving

The group around our dining room table was giddy with excitement. We stuffed down donuts and gulped steamy coffee as we congratulated ourselves on surprising Jack by waking him from a deep sleep to deliver his Christmas present. In the predawn hours on a South Florida Saturday, we revealed the plan to the still-sleepy recipient of our good will. Lisa and Lara and I had purchased a ride in a hot-air balloon for their dad. We had invited two of his best friends, Rick and Glenn, to join him. Glenn's wife, Gail, and Rick's fiancée, Kathy, completed our breakfast party.

Lisa and Lara danced around the table, laughing and clapping. "We did it!" they squealed. "We kept the secret!"

Jack pulled both girls into his lap, wrapping his big arms around them as they snuggled into his neck. I watched this high school hero of mine entwine our daughters with his love, and I couldn't believe how good our lives were. We'd been married over thirteen years, and despite some rough spots, we were living our dream of family, friends, church, community, two dogs, and a pool.

My reverie was broken by Glenn announcing that we'd better get going or we'd be late. We all piled into our station wagon and headed out to a suburban mall near Ft. Lauderdale. The parking lot, deserted so early in the morning, provided a great place to launch the balloon.

After inflating the massive folds of material into a billowing craft, the guys hopped into the basket with the pilot. The whoosh of the burner pushed heated air into the opening above their heads as they lifted off the ground. Gail, Kathy, the girls, and I watched and waved. Our own spirits were buoyant as the happy trio ascended.

Lisa and Lara climbed into the front seat of the car with me, and Gail and Kathy got in the back. We wove through streets parallel to the path of the balloon, vicariously enjoying the ride. We watched them glide over pastures and wave to grazing cattle in the few remaining fields outside the city. As they drifted near a housing development, I imagined the people waking up and seeing the festive red-and-white silk of the balloon lilting over their rooftops.

My attention was diverted from the adventurers and back to my driving. I had to maneuver around to get back on a street that ran parallel to their flight path. The balloon dropped momentarily out of sight behind some trees and reappeared as I turned the car onto a road that bordered a golf course.

Instantly joy was transformed into terror. A flame was burning through the wicker basket and licking up the sides. As the blaze curled up over the edge, Jack and the others began beating at the flames with their hands. Panic gripped us. We watched as two people leaped from the basket that was now a roaring furnace. I pulled the car off the road.

I pushed Lisa and Lara down onto the floor of the car to prevent them from seeing the horror around us and told them to stay in the car as I jumped out and ran toward the bodies lying on the golf course. Glenn and the pilot were sprawled motionless on the ground.

I knelt by Glenn softly asking him to somehow let me know if he heard me, but he didn't respond. I was lightly touching him and whispering in his ear when I heard the explosion. I looked up and saw only a fireball. I hadn't seen Jack and Rick fall, but I knew immediately that all of them were dead.

For one brief moment, in the midst of unthinkable pain, God surrounded me in a protective cocoon. I looked up at a crystal blue sky with a few white, billowy clouds creating an upward path. The reality of heaven filled me and blocked out the hoofbeats of the pale horse whose rider is Death. I wanted to go with Jack and the others.

The sight of my children erased my desire to enter heaven. They were standing by the front fender of the car, crying and waiting for me. I walked toward them with tears clouding my vision. They looked so small. At seven and ten years of age, they had just witnessed the death of their father. I knelt down and pulled them to me. We hugged and cried and began our long journey with loss.

People started to spill out of the houses that bordered the golf course. A man came up to me and asked what he could do to help. We all followed him to his house to use the phone to call one of our pastors. His wife met us at the door, still in her bathrobe. She immediately hugged Lisa and Lara and led me to the phone.

There were phone calls and policemen and journalists. I gratefully drank coffee and numbly answered questions. The pastor I had called finally arrived to take us home. The news of the accident had gone out over the radio, sending a shock wave through our neighborhoods and our church. Several dozen people were already at my house when we pulled up. One of the neighbors had gotten in, and the house was buzzing. The phone was ringing nonstop, more and more people arrived, and the girls and I were enveloped with love and concern. A steady stream of friends continued into the evening hours.

Several of my friends spent the night. Their husbands went home and got them nightgowns and clothes for the next day. These women never left me for a moment. As I started to go change for bed, someone asked me where my shoes were. I looked down and realized that I had taken them off before going into the couple's house where we used the phone. The grass on the golf course, wet with morning dew, had soaked my shoes. I hadn't remembered to get them again.

Four frazzled women stood in my kitchen looking at my bare feet. I felt silly and noticed that my feet were really dirty. I started to laugh, and they joined me. We hugged each other and tears mingled with smiles. No one washed my feet that night, but I felt like they did. Those dear friends filled the bedrooms of my house and the raw places of my heart with their presence. I went to bed alone for the first time in many years, but they were nearby. It made a difference.

In the next few days, all of our needs were met by others. Food, rides, arrangements for out-of-town people arriving for the memorial service—everything was covered. One friend offered to come over the morning of the service and get the girls dressed. She had two children and had been widowed a few years before. It was a welcome gift of service that would never have occurred to me. Another woman—I still don't know who—came in and took our laundry home. She washed it, folded it, and returned it. I couldn't imagine ever asking someone to wash my dirty clothes, but it was a wonderful gift.

I couldn't eat for the first three days. Friends tried coaxing me with a wide range of the abundant food that had been delivered. But I couldn't swallow anything solid. Then another woman, who had suffered the death of a child, brought over a clear broth. It smelled good and looked easy to get down. She, too, had been in the valley and felt the grip of a body knotted with shock. Her broth was the first nourishment I managed to swallow in those three days.

Tragic times often bring out the best in people, and that was certainly true when Jack died. Bountiful, generous giving comforted us and eased the transition into our new life. I look back and marvel at the willingness my friends displayed to have their own lives disrupted.

Many of them are still a part of my life, and they modestly profess that they didn't really do anything special. But my daughters and I know better. They gave and gave and gave. I know, too, that they would want me to acknowledge that the Source of their strength and love was the Source that filled me as I knelt on the golf course.

When Jack died, my daughters and I entered a season of receiving. Shock, loss, and grief consumed our energies and pierced our lives with overwhelming needs. For months, we continued to heal under the life-giving touches of many generous women.

While death and other events—divorce, illness, difficulty with children, aging parents—catapult people into positions of obvious need, some life stages lend themselves to seasons of receiving as well.

PREDICTABLE PERIODS FOR RECEIVING

Perhaps two of the most predictable times in our lives that are seasons of receiving are when we are the mothers of young children and when we or someone in our family is going through an illness.

I have a front-row seat to watch a mother with young children as I interact with my daughter Lisa and her two boys. Lisa participates in a women's Bible study which is comprised largely of young mothers, and they constantly pitch in to help each other. When my grandson Alex was born, I stayed with Lisa and Chadd for the first week and enjoyed the care of many of these women as they delivered wonderful meals, took Alex's older brother, Justin, for an afternoon of play, or stopped by just to give Lisa an audience for her delivery story. Lisa's fatigue was eased and her spirits lifted by being on the receiving end of generous giving.

Just last week I baby-sat for Justin and Alex for four days while Chadd and Lisa attended a wedding out of town. While I loved being with my grandsons, I was exhausted by the morning of day three. A friend to both Lisa and me, Cindy, called and offered to come over that afternoon for a few hours to give me a break. I almost declined her offer, feeling guilty at even wanting a break. But wisdom won out, and I gladly spent a few childless hours. I came back refreshed and better able to enjoy the remaining caregiving time.

Many of my friends are now facing the awesome responsibility of caring for ill and aging parents. Choosing nursing homes or other care facilities fills their time and drains their energies. I often hear these women express guilt over their inability to give or serve in other areas. But it's a season in their lives for receiving. They are giving in one particular area and need to accept the care of friends in others.

Another trying time in a woman's life when she will discover the need to receive is when menopause symptoms descend.

I interviewed over one hundred women when I wrote my book on women in midlife, with specific attention to the topic of menopause. Many life changes occur during the decades of our forties and fifties, but the physiological disruptions of menopause can catapult us into unfamiliar territory.

"I am undone," Fran told me. "I'm edgy and short-tempered, and I am so tired I could just sleep all day."

Fran's experience is typical. Any woman who lives long enough goes through menopause. It produces unexpected and often irritating symptoms. It crawls through our lives—sometimes for ten years.

But menopause eventually ends.

I was reminded during my own days of struggling with jangled emotions, fatigue, and hot flashes of the days when my children were toddlers. I remember daydreaming of a time when I could take a bath undisturbed or lavish in the luxury of reading a magazine from cover to cover. Now I relish my times with my grandbabies tugging on my sleeve and interrupting me. Life is a series of changes and seasons and cycles. This season won't last forever.

SELF-IMPOSED SEASONS OF GIVING

Sometimes we need self-imposed seasons of receiving. Perhaps our resources are drained, or we are struggling with something that requires us to spend more time in contemplation and rest.

Patricia is a generous woman who seems to roll through life. She has not endured any major tragedies, and she is grateful. But Patricia gets tired. She struggles with taking needed seasons of receiving because she feels she should be able to keep giving at the same pace all the time. But since her sixtieth birthday, Patricia has begun to slow down once in a while. She has begun taking mini-spiritual retreats, going away for an overnight in a hotel, just to rest and be with God. At first she was uncomfortable taking the time away from family and friends and spending the money, but her husband encouraged her to go. She has found these little getaways to be valuable in receiving care from her husband and replenishment from God.

Recently I met a woman in church leadership who told me that for the first time in over twenty years she has decided to step down from a leadership position. She told me nothing dramatic was happening in her life to cause added stress, but she just felt weary. I spoke with this veteran giver several months later, and she excitedly told me about some of the women who had stepped forward to fill the gap her absence created. "They might never have volunteered if I had stayed in leadership," she said. "I am relieved, and they are glad to be doing what they're doing."

Part of being a woman of a generous spirit includes receiving with gratitude and allowing others the benefit of reaching out in meaningful ways. Seasons of receiving for one person may open the door to a season of giving for another.

COMFORTING OTHERS AGAIN

The love and care I received when Jack died changed my life. I was carried and healed by God's direct touch and the wonderfully giving touches of others. Over the years God has used me to bring comfort and hope to others.

Last year I spoke to a group of widows. It was the first time in all these years that I was invited to address a group so specifically defined. The number of participants was not great; about one hundred women met at The Cove in Asheville, North Carolina. But it was one my most personally fulfilling weekends.

I met women who had been widowed as recently as two weeks prior to the conference and others who had been widowed for a number of years. The identification we had with one another was richly soothing. An atmosphere of tranquillity permeated our interaction. The comfort I received during the most devastating season of my life had been transformed into hope for other women.

Every trial we face and every season of receiving we travel through provide the soil for the seeds of future giving.

"Praise be to the God and Father of our Lord Jesus Christ, the Father of compassion and the God of all comfort, who comforts us in all our troubles, so that we can comfort those in any trouble with the comfort we ourselves have received from God. For just as the sufferings of Christ flow over into our lives, so also through Christ our comfort overflows" (2 Corinthians 1:3-5).

❧

We've just spent ten chapters gaining perspective on how to become women of a generous spirit. Before moving to the next section on the gifts we can give, I want to emphasize one thing: Becoming women of a generous spirit is an ongoing process. The characteristics in the last ten chapters will not be once-in-a-lifetime mountains that you successfully climb and then move on. You will work on these qualities your entire life.

You'll experience victories over unforgiveness or busyness or learn gracious communication and then slip back into your old ways. Take heart, and don't give up.

Now for the fun part. Section Two suggests a number of gifts we all can give. They don't depend on talent or performance. They spring from women whose hearts have been touched and filled and now overflow. Women like you.

Questions and Suggestions

1. Are you in a season of receiving now? If not, write a paragraph about a past season when you were in need.

2. If you are in a season of receiving, think about some changes

you may need to make. Let others know of your needs and begin to free yourself up.

3. Spend some time periodically (daily, weekly) writing down your feelings. They will change, and having a record of them will encourage you later as you review how God has moved during this time.

4. Spend time with a soul friend who lifts your spirits.

Section Two

❧

THE GIFTS
WE GIVE

Chapter 11

Grace

Plenty of people wish to become devout,
but no one wishes to be humble.

LA ROCHEFOUCAULD

"My grandparents were very gracious," Traci said wistfully. "They even financed my first car. I come from a very responsible family, and they told me I would have to pay them back with interest. Then I ran into financial trouble, and they kindly withdrew my debt."

Traci received the benefit of owning her own car, and her grandparents paid the price. One of the definitions I learned for *grace* is represented by the acrostic G-R-A-C-E: God's Riches At Christ's Expense. Christians enjoy the benefits of reconciled relationship with God, encompassing all the promises and rewards, because of Christ's paying for our sins on the cross. When we give grace, we bear an expense for others so that they may receive a benefit.

Of course, our sacrifices for other people are not comparable with God's sacrifice for us. The grace we extend to others pales when seen in the shadow of the cross. Jerry Bridges addresses this difference in his book *Transforming Grace*:

Grace is not only to be received by us, it is, in a sense, to be extended to others. I say "in a sense" because our relationship to other people is different from God's relationship to us. He is the infinitely superior Judge and moral Governor of the universe. We are all sinners and are on an equal plane with one another. So we cannot exercise grace as God does, but we can relate to one another as those who have received grace and who wish to operate on the principles of grace.[1]

Bridges goes on to explain that God's transforming grace is seen in expressions of gratitude, contentment, humility, forbearance, and forgiveness.[2] We can only give others grace when we have grasped what we have received from God and when we view others as our peers.

If we give with attitudes of self-importance or self-righteousness, we're in danger of elevating ourselves above those to whom we give. We may give expecting compensation for our graciousness—which negates the gift.

When Traci's grandparents erased her debt, they did it without fanfare and without reminders of how much they had helped her. They freed Traci from her obligation.

We can give grace from the overflow of God's immeasurable

love for us. "For it is by grace you have been saved, through faith—and this not from yourselves, it is the gift of God—not by works, so that no one can boast" (Ephesians 2:8-9). God initiated and provided the means of our reconciliation with him by giving his son's life in our place on the cross. We do nothing to merit our pardon; it is a gift.

Women of a generous spirit have grasped God's love. They give without keeping score—*you owe me* is not part of their vocabularies. They give humbly with no strings attached because they have already received their reward in their relationship with God. Therefore, they free the recipient from paying them back.

GRACE HAS NO RIGHTS

Grace-givers also choose to give up their rights, but they are not doormats. No one can bully them because they live in the context of their relationships with God. They understand that humility doesn't mean being a pushover. When they assume humble positions, they give from places of security and safety. Their rights have been solidly established by the cross. By their faith in Christ, they are in positions of regal inheritance. They know no one can take this away from them, and that security allows them to humbly defer to others. They are walking reflections of God's love.

I met a grace-giver recently while traveling on an overbooked flight. Passengers jammed the aisles as they struggled to drag carry-on luggage to their assigned, cramped slivers of space. As the boarding process was completed, a family of three charged into the coach-class cabin. A young father, mother, and infant were greeted by rows of unsympathetic eyes and almost audible prayers for this family to sit far away from the already entrenched travelers. I, too, hoped my weariness would not be further tested by the close proximity of a crying baby.

The father stopped a few rows in front of me and climbed into his center seat. His wife and infant struggled back to the row in front of mine. They, too, had been assigned a center seat. As the young woman began to squeeze her heavy load into her seat, her husband called to her to wait a minute.

He looked pleadingly at the woman in the aisle seat next to him and asked if she would mind trading places with his wife. The woman glanced up from her magazine with a simple shake of her head to indicate she would not consider giving up an aisle seat for a dreaded, crushing three-hour experience in a center seat. I didn't blame her, even though I felt sorry for these parents.

An older woman in the aisle seat of the young wife's row stood up and quietly said something to the young father. He beamed a smile of gratitude and began to gather his belongings. His seat partner continued to show disdain at another disturbance.

I watched all of this with admiration for the graciousness of the older woman who willingly placed herself in a position of discomfort for the good of someone she didn't even know.

Grace-givers, like this older woman, choose to give what is theirs. They understand that if they've been hurt and treated badly, they have a right to feel offended. But they often choose to exchange their offended feelings for attitudes of grace. Even when they feel negatively toward others, they remember God's grace toward them. His love freed them, and they can choose to love others with similar grace.

One of my dearest friends, Marian, exemplifies this. I have known her and her family for almost twenty-three years. She is so aware of her relationship with God that she views all of life through the lens of his love. In difficulty and ease, she appropriates that love with the power to live and give graciously.

Marian longs for others to know Jesus and to feel his love through her. I don't recall a time when I have seen her respond to others in defense of her own position. Some have viewed Marian as being too soft, too kind, too giving, too quick to let others offend her. But she simply doesn't take offense. What some women might receive as rudeness, Marian sees as an indication of a need for love. She diffuses arguments and confrontations by giving others the benefit of the doubt.

When accused of some unkindness, she thoughtfully tries to see the perspective of the other person. She admits to her own shortcomings and seeks solutions instead of defending her point of view.

If Marian had been on the flight with the young family, she would have leaped up to help. Sitting in the middle seat would not have even seemed a sacrifice to her because she would have placed herself in the position of the young mother and sympathized with her need.

Her life illustrates Colossians 3:12: "Therefore, as God's chosen people, holy and dearly loved, clothe yourselves with compassion, kindness, humility, gentleness and patience." Marian wears these gracious garments wherever she goes. She thinks well of others all the way from the core of her being and reflects that attitude with continually gracious acts.

Most of us are not as deeply loving as Marian, and we will be offended when our rights are threatened. How we respond depends on how we view ourselves and how we view others. If we see ourselves as dearly loved daughters of the king, full of his provision in our lives, and if we see others as people created in his image who are in need of his love . . . maybe we can begin to respond with graciousness instead of demanding our own way.

Part of my journey in becoming a more generous woman is learning to give grace when others treat me rudely. I get indignant when I sense my rightful position being threatened. Just the other day I was in line at the grocery checkout counter and hesitated momentarily to move my cart forward. Another shopper slyly aimed her cart toward the space between me and the person in front of me. I quickly and defiantly shoved my cart forward and closed any gap in the line. My icy expression silently told the would-be line-crasher that I did *not* appreciate her attempt to steal what was rightfully mine.

Then there are the drivers who try to cut me off or ride my tail or dawdle in the passing lane. And I hate it when people don't look before walking and bump right into me. Of course, there are those who talk too loud and disrupt my own conversations or crawl over my seat in the middle of a movie.

I have my rights! I say in an attempt to justify my attitude.

But I am consciously trying to stop when I feel annoyed and ask God for the grace to respond with kindness.

GRACE HAS AN OPEN HEART

Lynn described another characteristic of a grace-giver as, "Someone who looks for opportunities to give. They have their eye out for giving. It's part of their attitude to notice things." This kind of generosity is foreign to many today. Not only do we often close our eyes and miss opportunities to extend grace, but we have become content to live in isolation; we're annoyed by interruptions.

When I was growing up, friends would often drop by near dinnertime and join us for our meal. We often did the same. We might be out and stop by someone's house and find ourselves laughing and talking over dinner with them. My mother always fixed extra food and enjoyed serving anyone who showed up. Society valued giving what was rightfully one's own to others for their well-being or pleasure. Sharing with a willing attitude was not uncommon.

Today interrupting a family at dinnertime is considered

impolite. We don't interrupt others in their sanctuaries, and we don't want to be interrupted. Certainly frequent interruptions would be intrusive. It's considerate to call ahead and to respect people's need for privacy. But one unfortunate result of our society's value of independence is a lack of awareness of natural ways to extend graciousness. When a doorbell rings unexpectedly, we can answer with warmth. We can invite people in. If it really is an inconvenient time for them to visit, we can apologize for not being able to spend time with them and set up another time. But if there is any way to transform their interruption into an opportunity for relationship—invite them to pull up a chair.

Grace requires touching others. It motivates us to look for ways to include others. Jesus left heaven to give the gift of his grace to us. We, in turn, need to consider if isolation is preventing others from experiencing gracious giving from us.

An open heart reveals attitudes of grace in much the same way an open door reveals attitudes of hospitality. We are able to unlock our hearts as we grasp the fullness we experience in our relationship with God. We don't need to fear being insulted, taken advantage of, or being walked on because we are not easily offended. If others are rude, intrusive, or inconsiderate, we are better able to smile and extend attitudes that reflect those attitudes we experience from God. We are able to step aside, move over, and embrace all kinds of people just because we want to show them love.

Steve and I went to see the movie *Shine* when it was first

released. We were in a sparkling, new theater with a steeply elevated floor and lots of room between rows. The chair backs were well above our heads and luxuriously comfortable.

We settled in with anticipation of seeing a great movie. During much of the movie, the lead character is playing a difficult Rachmaninoff piece on the piano. As he grows up, his playing improves, and the movie audience hears more and more of his performances.

The tapping on the back of my chair began with light touches and escalated as the character's performances improved. Soon my seat was being enthusiastically kicked by the woman behind me. Steve's seat started to rock in unison with mine. We waited, hoping she would realize what she was doing and stop.

Finally Steve turned around and asked her to please stop kicking my seat. I turned enough to see the startled look on her face and hear her genuinely apologize.

We sat undisturbed until near the end of the movie. Then during the final concert performance, the kicking began again. This time it was restrained. My seat bopped gently to the beat, and I peeked back through the crack between the seats to see the woman gazing euphorically at the screen.

Steve looked at me as his own seat began to rock, and we smiled. We silently agreed to allow this enraptured music lover to enjoy the few remaining moments undisturbed.

I am probably guilty of pride for including this story, but my intent is to highlight how good it felt for me to waive my own rights for the benefit of another. My usual response was, and is, to ask a seat-kicker to please stop. I think that it's okay to graciously ask people to respect certain physical boundaries. But when I saw what the music meant to this stranger, I found myself enjoying being part of her experience. I love piano music, but it obviously meant a great deal more to her than to me. What began as an offense was transformed into an opportunity for giving grace to her and receiving fulfillment for me.

CREATING SAFE PLACES FOR OTHERS

Grace also gives people a place to make mistakes.

I have been with my friend Marian and watched her turn an offender into a friend. She creates safe places for people to be offensive and still be treated with love. Someone can try to jostle her out of her place in a line, and she just moves over and invites them to move in front of her. Before long, they are engaged in conversation, and the intruder is smiling and thanking Marian. Those people may never know that Marian treats them that way because of her relationship with God, but at least they do experience grace from another human being.

When I was a little girl, I was appendage challenged. My arms and legs grew much faster than my ability to control them. I was always bumping into doorframes and counter corners and knocking over clearly visible items.

My father had little tolerance for this kind of carelessness, so I often found myself in trouble for my repeated mistakes. I was reminded of my clumsiness in a scene from the movie *Regarding Henry*. Harrison Ford plays a high-powered attorney who suffers a brain injury that results in his need to learn simple tasks all over again. He struggles to talk, walk, and adapt to everyday life. In one particular scene, he is eating breakfast with his wife and young daughter. His daughter accidentally knocks over a full glass of orange juice.

As I watched the glass tumble over, my stomach knotted in anticipation of the scolding she would receive. I had been notorious for knocking over glasses as a child, and I got yelled at every time.

Harrison Ford looked at his daughter and then smiled at her and knocked over his own glass of juice. His daughter was pleasantly surprised at her formerly strict father's affirming response. I cried. I could not imagine what it would have been like to make a mistake and receive that kind of gracious response.

I know my father wanted to teach me to be more responsible, but I learned to be hypervigilant instead. I didn't have a safe place to make mistakes. A spilled glass of juice can be a small offense that carries a big impact. People suffer from all kinds of greater failures that follow them through life. They may have made mistakes as parents, been disappointed in careers, missed success in school, and feel ashamed and discouraged.

Grace treats others in ways that encourage them to relax, to be themselves, to learn and grow. Grace motivates them to try again and not be afraid to make another mistake.

Sometimes our greatest challenge in giving grace is to give it to those we love.

GRACE IN OUR CLOSES RELATIONSHIPS

"Above all, love each other deeply, because love covers over a multitude of sins. Offer hospitality to one another without grumbling. Each one should use whatever gift he has received to serve others, faithfully administering God's grace in its various forms" (1 Peter 4:8-10).

Loving each other deeply is easier than it may sound. The closer we get to others and the closer they get to us, the more we scrape each other with our rough edges. We've all experienced the difference between our expectations of living with someone and the reality of actually doing it. Whether with a spouse, children, parents, or friends, our ability to show grace to constant companions can diminish over time.

Women of a generous spirit hold back judgment and engage their loved ones in ways that communicate love. Kindness, humility, respect—all go a long way in being able to talk with people about living with them in ways that are beneficial for everyone. Of course, we'll all get angry and spout off unkind words. But those instances should be the exception and not the rule. And when we make mistakes or treat others disrespectfully, we need to apologize to them and evaluate what made us angry in the first place.

Grace doesn't mean that we stuff our feelings, but that we communicate in ways that reflect love, not judgment. I remember listening to a friend tell a Bible study about her struggle with office devotions. She explained that she worked for a Christian organization that had corporate, weekly devotions and departmental, daily devotions. Employees rotated as facilitators of the morning spiritual time which lasted about fifteen minutes.

"There we were," Jane said, "sitting around talking about God and how to live the Christian life. Then as soon as devotions were over, we acted just like people who didn't know him at all. We were competitive and gossipy and always looking out for ourselves."

Sometimes we treat those most important to us with the least care. We take them for granted and feel little need to be humble or to give up what is rightfully ours. These fluctuating emotions that bounce back and forth between grace and judgment are normal, but women of a generous spirit monitor them. Grace-givers are slow to judge others. They give people the benefit of the doubt until something happens to prove otherwise.

Attitudes of grace give others room to relate with God personally and apply his truth in their lives as they discern his leading. Givers of grace also recognize that they are not infallible—they can make mistakes in judgment and misunderstand the hearts of other brothers and sisters in Christ.

Steve and I recently asked George Verwer, President of Operation Mobilisation, what he felt American believers needed most. George and his wife have lived in London for a number of years and travel extensively all over the world. They are Americans with family still living here, but they have the advantage of seeing us from a broad, yet godly, perspective.

Without hesitation, George responded, "Grace!"

He went on to say that it saddened him to visit the United States and see so much harsh judgment among believers. We often don't see the equality of fallenness we all share. Instead of extending gracious love to others, especially in the family of believers, we respond unkindly. We are often not safe in each other's company.

Grace is a gift of attitude. We can fake gracious actions, but if we aren't giving from hearts overflowing with God's love, our actions won't be life-giving. Authentic grace is an awareness of our own guilt paid for by Christ and a desire to extend that love to others.

Gifts of grace call people into relationship with each other and with God. They provide safe places for failure, forgiveness, and growth.

Questions and Suggestions

1. Write down how you naturally respond when offended.

2. Consider how you might change your response to demonstrate the reality of God's grace in your life.

3. How are you filling up in your relationship with God?

4. What do you need to consider changing to better experience his fullness?

5. Do you consider yourself a safe place for others to make mistakes? Why or why not?

6. Do you feel that you live a somewhat isolated life? Why or why not?

7. Write down four words that you would like others to think of when asked to describe you. Are you reflecting those values now?

8. Determine that this week you will respond with grace in a situation where your rights are infringed upon. Write a paragraph to describe the encounter.

9. Think of some ways in which you are uniquely gifted (mercy, hospitality, administration, etc.). Are there some ways you might extend grace by expressing your gifts? Example: If you are gifted in acts of mercy, you could give up an afternoon to visit someone in the hospital or baby-sit for a friend with no return obligation; if you are gifted in administration, you could volunteer to help someone or an organization in need of your skills.

Chapter 12

Hope

If it were not for hope, the heart would break.

THOMAS FULLER

My mother called one Sunday afternoon and asked me to come over and look at a sore on her foot that was beginning to worry her. As I drove over, my heart raced with the anticipation of finding ravaging results of my mother's diabetes. When I arrived, she was propped up in bed with her foot elevated. My father looked frightened as he nervously rearranged medications on the nightstand. Obviously they had been trying to diagnose and treat an ailment that should have been immediately tended by a doctor.

A cut on the bottom of her big toe oozed the deadly, black pus that screamed the evidence of gangrene. I felt sick as I looked at her foot, knowing it was too late. I called her doctor, and we met him at the hospital within the hour. My mother was admitted and began a grueling nine-week process of amputations that began with the removal of one toe, then all toes, and finally the amputation of her leg.

My mother was told that not only had she lost her leg, but that she would never walk again. The doctor explained that a woman of her age and weight could not expect to navigate on an artificial leg. It would simply be too difficult for her to learn to wear a prosthesis.

While my mother wisely held no hope for the restoration of her amputated limb, she did dream that one day she could walk again. During her rehabilitation, encouraging nurses—angels of mercy— gave her hope. These wonderful women talked to my mother as they taught her how to move from bed to wheelchair and back to bed. They whispered that she *could* manage a prosthesis. Several of the nurses were women of faith, and they talked to my mother about God's power to help her. My daughter Lara sat on Mother's bed and talked to her about Jesus helping her walk. My mother spoke little about her faith but did tell Lara she believed in Jesus and in his power.

Despite her doctor's pessimism, he wrote her a prescription and made an appointment for her to visit a lab in Denver to be fitted for an artificial leg. For two months we drove back and forth to the lab where my mother endured painful lessons on how to walk with her artificial leg. The practitioners at the lab cheered her on with words of encouragement and praise. At each visit they painted a verbal picture of her walking unassisted across a room.

She embellished the vision by dreaming of walking to greet Lisa, my other daughter, when she came home from college for Thanksgiving break. Her faith, her hope of seeing Lisa's face as she walked toward her, and the loving support and prompting of the lab staff kept my mother going.

Thanksgiving morning came, and my parents drove up our driveway. Lisa started to run out to the car, but Lara held her back. My mother got out of the car and walked up the front path. She put out her arms and wrapped her granddaughter in a warm embrace. Tears trickled down both their faces as my mother's hopes became reality.

After my mother's surgery, she was told she would never walk again. With the help and the vision of others, she was able to believe that another reality existed just out of sight.

Givers of hope see what others can be and do with God's touch operating in their lives. They know that godly hope is not denial. It accepts reality but brings the supernatural truth of the power of God into every situation: Loss and danger are not faced alone; God and other believers walk with the fearful through the valleys of pain.

Hope is not a reflection of powerlessness but of faith in a power apart from ourselves. Hope in God's love frees us from the delusion that we can save ourselves.

Hope increases our willingness to risk living as God wants us to live.

HOPE BELIEVES THE BEST

Hope encourages those whose vision is blurred by the gray clouds of discouragement and disappointment. Hope whispers: *You are loved.*

The intensity of pain will lessen. I believe in you. The burden of one is carried by both.

Linda and Michelle have been friends for over ten years. They love and care for each other and are mutual sources of hope. Linda told me how Michelle recently lifted her spirits. "I had received a call from my son's school. Brad was in trouble again and in danger of being suspended. His dad was out of town, so I had to go alone to the principal's office to receive their decision on how to handle his latest offense.

"Every time Brad gets in trouble, I sink lower and lower and lose hope that he will ever change. We've tried everything, but he just doesn't respond. It's a heavy hurt that I carry all the time."

Michelle helps Linda with the reality that her son may not change, while reminding her that Brad is only sixteen and could change at any time. The uncertainty is maddening, but Linda has hope when she talks with Michelle. Michelle doesn't judge her as a parent and loves Brad, despite his rebellious ways. "I can trust her with my hurts," Linda said. "She is my sounding board. I don't know what I'd do without her listening ear and wise words. I feel like such a failure, and Michelle helps me see that I still have value even though this is happening to us."

It's easy to slip into hopelessness when faced with the reality of living with continual pain. God uses women who are experiencing his fullness to touch our aching souls with his love and remind us that we are loved. Hope often comes when the overflowing love from one woman replenishes the dwindling supply in another. Then, in the ebb and flow of life, the gift of hope can be returned. Even women who experience great fullness in their relationship with God suffer discouragement and disappointment. They, too, need hope.

"Michelle never gives me pie-in-the-sky advice," Linda told me. "She listens and expresses her own sorrow for me and points me back to God's unconditional love. She doesn't spout off verses but just talks softly, encouraging me to believe I really am an okay person despite how I feel at the moment. Other times, Michelle calls me with her own disappointment, and I try to listen and encourage her."

Hope. What would we do without it?

HANG ON TO HOPE

When I feel discouraged or disappointed, I don't automatically rejoice. I sit for a while in my misery. I run painful images through my brain about whatever is troubling me. If this continues, I swirl down a funnel, feeling hopelessness.

Recently I picked up a book called *Emotional Resilience* by David Viscott, M.D., thinking it might contain some helpful tidbits about hope. This is what I found:

Hope interferes with the natural healing process by leading you to expect to be saved and thus to postpone saving yourself.

When you have hope, you're really in denial. You are insisting: things aren't as bad as they seem; things will get better, the other person will change or will love you again someday. You should accept the truth as soon as possible and make adjustments.

Typically you count on hope when you're the most afraid. You are going to have to face the loss or danger by yourself anyway—why lose time hoping for things to get better while they only get worse?

Hope is the reflection of powerlessness, a child's cry for its mother to deliver him in the face of the fearful unknown.

Hope has destroyed more lives than any other emotion, by thwarting the normal instinct to save yourself.

Hope keeps you from growing.

Give up hope.[1]

I read those words and initially felt angry. Then I read them again and felt sad that anyone would embrace such a desolate conclusion about that which infuses power into our lives and enables us to overcome our discouragement and disappointment. I was even able to thank the author for jolting me out of my tendency to wallow in my pain instead of seizing my negative thoughts and bringing them under the influence of God's Word and his Spirit.

Hope which is rooted in God makes a difference in our lives. Such living hope doesn't deny that bad things are bad and may not get better, but it willingly opens our hearts and minds to God's transforming comfort today and the promise of an eternal inheritance tomorrow.

Women like Linda and Michelle give hope by talking, listening, and reminding each other that their discouragement and disappointment don't have the power to destroy them. Pain and trials may intrude into their lives, but hoping in God's goodness and love empowers them to live in fullness.

Hang on to hope.

SEEING BENEATH THE SURFACE

"When I think of women of a generous spirit," Jan said, "I think of a friend of mine.

"When people speak about her, they always speak of how she has impacted their lives. For me, she has a vision of who I can be. She dreams for me, thinks about who I am now and who I can be. She knows I have a lot to give, and if she isn't getting that from me, she will call it to my attention.

"She energizes me and disrupts me and makes me uncomfortable in a wonderful way. She touches me because she is willing to be with me in my hurt, but she knows the hurt itself is not the bottom line. The bottom line is what I am going to do with the hurt. She weeps with me and has a vision for the ton of beauty that is going to come out of the pain."

Jan went on to tell me that she longs to be married and, at thirty-three, sometimes loses hope in that dream. "My friend dreams of the kind of woman I will be if I keep my heart open. But she also dreams deeply of my being married and that I would not close off my heart and hide in the marriage. She keeps me looking to God."

We see most clearly that which is right in front of us. Jan sees her singleness while her friend sees Jan's heart and God's possibilities for her. Jan is encouraged by the hope held carefully for her by another.

Sometimes we are faced with hoping in the midst of seemingly unchanging circumstances; other times we are faced with believing that our dreams may actually be answered. We are called to see beneath the surface. God is working in mysterious ways in our lives and hearts.

HOPE THAT TRANSCENDS THIS LIFE

John Donne wrote, "Any man's death diminishes me, because I am involved in mankind; and therefore never send to know for whom the bell tolls; it tolls for thee."

We will all face the ultimate robber of hope: death. But for women of a generous spirit, death is only a temporary valley through which we pass to arrive at a most hopeful destination. Death is still dreaded and sweeps us into the pain of separation from loved ones, but it is not our final reality. In his first letter Peter reminds us of our ultimate hope:

> *In his great mercy he has given us new birth into a living*
> *hope through the resurrection of Jesus Christ from the dead,*
> *and into an inheritance that can never perish, spoil or fade—*
> *kept in heaven for you, who through faith are shielded by*
> *God's power until the coming of the salvation that is ready to*
> *be revealed in the last time. In this you greatly rejoice, though*
> *now for a little while you may have had to suffer grief in all*
> *kinds of trials. (1 Peter 1:3-6)*

The most life-giving hope we have and can offer to others is the hope of eternal life. Nothing can rob those who know Jesus of this amazing gift. And unlike all other comforts, the reality of living forever transcends death. The bell will toll for us, but it ushers us into a new world.

Years ago I went to visit a dying friend. Rod Sargent, a former vice president with the Navigators, was suffering through his final mortal moments in a battle with cancer. I had asked his wife, Diane, if I could just slip in and say good-bye. She explained that he was unable to respond, and it was uncertain if he was aware of any who came to see him, but I was welcome to come.

I drove up to their house with my tongue jammed against the roof of my mouth. Someone had taught me long ago that such pressure can often prevent tears from spilling out. I was determined to see Rod without breaking down. I didn't want to upset Diane or make a scene. How silly.

Rod was in a bed in a darkened room of their home, lying with eyes closed and no signs of movement. Diane pulled up a chair by his bed and left the room. As I sat down, the tears flowed. I touched Rod's hand and softly spoke.

"Thank you for your kindness to me and for treating me with respect," I said to one of the few men I knew involved in ministry fund-raising who communicated care for donors, not just interest in their giving potential.

Rod didn't move. His breathing was shallow and his color chalk-like. I don't know if he heard me, but I felt like I heard him. I sensed that without saying a word he was telling me he knew he was going to a wonderful place. He had little time left to be trapped in pain and was on his way to a great adventure.

Dietrich Bonhoeffer wrote from prison, "Death is the supreme festival on the road to freedom."[2] We seldom think of death as freedom, but as I sat by Rod on what turned out to be the last day of his earthly life, I saw a man about to be free. The valley of the shadow is painful and frightening, but it is temporary. Life on the other side in paradise is forever.

I cannot speak to anyone about heaven without crying. My tears are not tears of hopelessness, they are tears of sadness at the loss we live with when we are the ones left behind. While we live with pain this side of heaven, our hope is grounded in the reality that our loved ones are alive in a perfect place and we are headed there too.

Without hope, we will eventually be truly hopeless. If death is the end, then the most flamboyantly lived life screeches to a halt against the wall of obliteration. Gifts of eternal hope are given by written and spoken words and music that remind us of what lies ahead. When we breathe even a scent of the mystical fragrance of heaven, we are filled with the overflowing hope of God's love in its most dramatically life-giving way.

Then I saw a new heaven and a new earth, for the first heaven and the first earth had passed away, and there was no longer any sea. I saw the Holy City, the new Jerusalem, coming down out of heaven from God, prepared as a bride beautifully dressed for her husband. And I heard a loud voice from the throne saying, "Now the dwelling of God is with men, and he will live with them. They will be his people, and God himself will be with them and be their God. He will wipe every tear from their eyes. There will be no more death or mourning or crying or pain, for the old order of things has passed away."

He who was seated on the throne said, "I am making everything new!" (Revelation 21:1-5)

The hope we have as Christians—relationship with God and his help and presence in this life and an eternal future in heaven—transcends death. What an unspeakable gift to give to others. Givers of hope encourage others when times are tough or the future is uncertain. And then when prayers are answered, we get to share in the joy.

WHEN HOPE IS REALIZED

Devlin and Carol began adoption procedures over three years ago. Because they were attempting an international adoption, they expected complications that could delay the process. Maria was born in Ecuador in September of 1995. Devlin and Carol, still in the midst of frustrating paperwork, were notified that this little girl might be the perfect match for them. They received pictures of this tiny princess and instantly fell in love. Our home group, of which Devlin and Carol are a part, began to pray for Maria and her expedient arrival in Colorado. Little did we know that it would be early 1997 before Maria and her new parents would be united.

During those long months, we shared the disappointing delays with Devlin and Carol. We lingered over snapshots of Maria as she grew from an infant into an adorable toddler. We all hoped and prayed that the adoption would actually transpire, but there were times when that looked doubtful. Our little group, and many other friends of Devlin and Carol, encouraged them to keep their hearts hopeful.

They finally boarded a plane bound for Ecuador to pick up Maria and bring her home. When the three of them arrived back at the Colorado Springs airport, an enthusiastic crowd greeted them with banners, applause, tears, and shouts of welcome.

One of the rewards of being a giver of hope is sharing in the joy when hopes become realities. Maria was baptized recently, and the vision we all carried in our minds and hearts for months stood before us: Devlin and Carol receiving God's blessing on their little girl, Maria, in the presence of those who love them.

HOPEFUL TOUCHES

Givers of hope are the cheerleaders in our lives. They encourage us to keep going, keep trying, never give up, while accepting us as we are. They let us know we're okay now, and they entice us to believe what we can become. What a combination!

Hope overcomes fear. It is the voice of God's promise that he will complete us, he has plans for us, he loves us, he is with us. He whispers those hopeful truths when we meet with him, and he speaks through those who cheer us on. They inspire us to move through our fears to see that pastures of peace are available. Even though circumstances might not change, God is active and involved in our lives. Hope in his character and goodness provide the ground for him to pour spiritual, life-giving love into hurting lives.

Women of a generous spirit bring that message to others and walk with them toward hope that becomes reality.

Questions and Suggestions

1. Write about any areas in your life where you feel hopeless.

2. Talk with a trusted woman friend about it and ask her to pray for you to change your focus from the present discouragement to what God can do in you.

3. Write down some names of women you know who need encouragement. Then begin to pray for them and for insightful ways to touch them.

4. How are you feeling about your relationship with God? Do you need to more effectively go to the source?

5. Schedule a morning or afternoon sometime in the next two weeks to spend a few hours with the Lord, focusing on restoring your own hope.

6. Write a note of encouragement to someone.

Chapter 13

Presence

> *We do not mind our not arriving anywhere*
> *nearly so much as our not having any company on the way.*
>
> FRANK MOORE COLBY

Women of a generous spirit know that just their physical presence can lighten the burden for another. Gifts of presence give the comfort of touch, compassion, and love to those in pain.

God's command to Joshua to be strong and courageous was based on God's presence: "Be strong and courageous. Do not be terrified; do not be discouraged, for the LORD your God will be with you wherever you go" (Joshua 1:9). God didn't tell Joshua to be strong and courageous because nothing difficult was going to happen. God's presence allowed Joshua to rise above the circumstances and be the man God called him to be.

Lara and I recently made a trip back East and visited the campus of the University of Maryland. I had been a student there years ago and was eager to show Lara the sorority house where I had lived.

As we walked through the living room and up the stairs to the bedrooms, memories of great times with wonderful friends came flooding back. We lived together and were there for each other. I remember one of the girls actually moving back into the house after she married to have the moral support of close friends. Her husband was serving in Vietnam and had been reported missing-in-action. Just a few days after she received the news, she moved out of her apartment and in with us. We couldn't change her situation, but she received comfort from being in our presence. We waited with her in fearful yet hopeful expectation. When the telegram came that he had been found and was okay, we rejoiced with her.

When our presence is life-giving, it touches others physically, emotionally, and spiritually. We wrap our arms around a friend or lay a hand on top of another trembling hand and silently place that person before God. We absorb some of their pain and feel a little of what they feel so dramatically.

People who live without the life-giving touch of another will tell you about the pain of aloneness. "I've been divorced for over three years now," Alice said, "and I could just scream from lack of physical contact. You'd think I have some kind of disease or something. No one hugs me or touches me. I feel terribly lonely and down."

Alice is a member of a large church and teaches Sunday school. She has lots of friends and a busy life. But she is alone in a crowd. She longs for someone to notice and reach out to her. "Someone told me," Alice continued, "that every person needs eight hugs a day to feel loved. Eight a day! I haven't had one hug in weeks."

Women of a generous spirit are sensitive to those who yearn for a caring touch. They are not intrusive but know how to squeeze a hand in greeting or lightly rest a hand on a shoulder in acknowledgment. With those they know, hugs are frequent.

We all know it feels good to be in the presence of caring people who touch us appropriately physically as well as emotionally and spiritually. We are emotionally touched when someone else hurts as a result of our pain. We can see concern in their eyes and hear compassion in their voices. They bring to life the old saying: *When one cries, the other tastes salt.*

Givers of presence know how to sit for hours with hurting people to bring the comfort of compassion into painful areas. In waiting rooms and at bedsides, people sit with each other and pass the poignant moments together. As my friend Corky works in the pediatric ward of the hospital, she gives her presence. She volunteers to be with parents whose children are ill. She listens to them, cries with them, prays with them, and helps the fearful time pass more comfortably.

When we give the gift of presence, we communicate to others that they are important enough for us to give time just to be with them. It costs us, but the life-giving results are worth it.

COUNTING THE COST OF OUR PRESENCE

Sir Thomas Browne said, "By compassion, we make others' misery our own." We pay the price of inviting pain into our lives when we give the gift of presence to those in pain. It costs us the intrusion of sadness, loss, and fear into our emotions. We may find ourselves drained and weary, our schedules shattered.

When a friend's life is interrupted by a painful situation, our lives are interrupted too. We lay aside our own agendas to be with that person. Illness is probably one of the most demanding crises any of us faces. Whether illness strikes us or someone we love, our routines are dashed and a myriad of emotions rush in. We may experience physical pain, fear, or doubt. The presence of others brings great comfort and comes at a price for the giver.

But women of a generous spirit know that a far greater price was paid for them. "You are not your own; you were bought at a price" (1 Corinthians 6:19-20). The price was the life of God's son so that we may be reconciled to God and be in relationship with him.

Women of a generous spirit come to hurting people full of the reality of the presence of God in their lives. They are, in turn, able and willing to interrupt their own lives to give their presence to others.

Vicki and Ellie had been friends for years when Ellie was diagnosed with breast cancer. Vicki was a physical, emotional, and spiritual presence throughout Ellie's long ordeal with this dreaded disease. Vicki often took Ellie for chemotherapy treatments and sat by her bed when the side effects kicked in. Both women talked of the hope of full recovery, and Vicki cried with Ellie at the possibility that recovery might not occur.

After several years Ellie began to lose her battle. As she lay quietly close to death, Vicki kept constant vigil. Day and night Vicki alternated shifts with Ellie's husband so that someone she loved was always with her.

"It took so much out of me," Vicki said after Ellie was gone, "but I didn't want to be anywhere else. I know my being there made a difference to Ellie, so that made a difference to me."

Gifts of presence call the giver into pain and the receiver into comfort. God mysteriously holds up both of them, even in the most painful circumstances. "I leaned on God more than ever," Vicki said. "Even when I was completely exhausted, I would come home and just sit with God. I needed his touch on my life to have anything left to give to Ellie. He was there; he came through."

INVITING OTHERS INTO OUR PRESENCE

So far in this chapter we've been looking at how women are present with others in pain. People also need the presence of others to enjoy the good times and share in the dailiness of life.

I first met Susan almost twenty years ago. She was single, and my first husband was still alive. Susan and I hit it off immediately and began to do things together. Jack was great about watching Lisa and Lara so that Susan and I could catch a movie or go shopping.

On one particular Saturday night we were having several couples over for a barbecue. I invited Susan to join us, and she readily accepted. There were nine of us around the dinner table enjoying a lively conversation and a lot of laughter.

After dinner, Susan was helping me load the dishwasher and quietly said, "I had a fabulous time, but where is he?"

"Where is who?" I asked her in bewilderment.

"The guy—you know, the blind date you must have invited to even out the number of people at dinner," she said quite seriously.

"Susan, there is no guy. I didn't invite a guy for you."

Tears welled up in her eyes as she smiled over the rack of dishes dripping with barbecue sauce.

"You mean that you invited me, just for me?"

"Yes. It never occurred to me to 'even out the number at the dinner table.'"

I learned that night through Susan, and later in my own experience as a widow, that many people think there is an eleventh unwritten commandment that says, "Thou shalt not have an uneven number of people around your dinner table."

I was unaware of the impact that night would have on my friendship with Susan. I stumbled onto something that women of a generous spirit know: People want to be valued for their individual presence. They want to know they have something to offer irrespective of their marital status or profession or abilities—just who they are makes them worthy of inclusion.

There are so many people that the gift of presence can touch. Inviting them into our lives to share a meal, a trip to the mall, or a phone conversation can give life in ways that communicate love.

Mary was widowed many years ago and is now an empty-nester. All of her children are grown and married. "It's just me and Andy," Mary said. "He's my dog. The other night I was so tired of eating alone that I took Andy in the car with me to the McDonald's drive-through. I ordered two hamburgers and one order of fries—Andy doesn't eat fries. I pulled the car over to a parking space in the far corner of the lot, and we each ate a burger. I had dinner with my dog."

Many people long for the gift of presence. Women of a generous spirit keep an eye out for those who are alone and intentionally get to know them and invite them just to have fun with them.

Sometimes no matter how many caring friends fill our lives, we'll find ourselves alone. But we are only alone humanly speaking. God's presence is a constant in our lives.

REMINDING OURSELVES OF GOD'S PRESENCE

We live in a very sense-oriented society. Because of our exposure to such extreme sensual stimulation, it's challenging to be aware of the presence of someone who is not defined by our physical senses. God is with us, but sometimes it's hard to feel as if he is. We don't see him with our eyes or hear him with our ears or touch him with our hands. We see, hear, and touch him in our spirits—with our hearts. He comes to us as Spirit.

Awareness of his presence is part of the filling he gives women of a generous spirit. They meet with him, and they take him with them out into the world. He lives in them, and they are aware of that reality. His presence fills them up and allows them to give with power.

The more we meet with him and get to know him, the more able we will be to experience the reality of the presence of God in our lives. He is in us now, but our awareness will grow as our relationship with him deepens. It will become second nature to stop and acknowledge the God of comfort being present at any and every moment.

I was baby-sitting for Justin one day not long after he had learned to walk. We were in the living room, and he was pulling toys out of his toy box. I was leafing through a magazine while sitting on the couch. Since he could maneuver across the room on his own, he didn't want me fussing over him all the time. He was enjoying his newfound independence that coordination brings.

I got up and went into the kitchen to get a drink without saying anything to him. I was just around the corner but out of his line of vision. As soon as I stopped by the refrigerator, I noticed the silence. Justin was no longer pulling out toys; he was still. I waited momentarily before peeking around to see what he was up to. But before I could move, he called to me. "Nana?"

"I'm right here, Buddy," I quickly replied. "Nana's in the kitchen."

Then I could hear his little feet patter across the carpet heading in my direction. He came around the corner and stopped as he smiled broadly at me.

"Nana," he sighed in relief.

I patted his back as he hugged my leg and assured him that I would never leave him, that he was okay because his Nana was with him. He gazed up at me with those sparkling blue eyes, and life was sweet. My presence mattered in this little one's life, and my desire was to be nowhere else at that moment but with him.

Wouldn't it be wonderful if we, like little children, could stop when God slips out of our spiritual vision and call to him. To quietly pause in the middle of our hectic lives and in our spirits speak his name—*Jesus*—then wait for just a moment for him to affirm his presence to us.

The gift of God's presence is ours. It fills us with comfort and assurance of his love. It propels us to go and give the gift of our presence—and his—to others.

Questions and Suggestions

1. What women have been present with you during difficult times? How were they there for you?

2. With whom—and how—have you been present with others during difficult times?

3. Write down your feelings about the interruption that prolonged periods of being present create.

4. In what ways do you feel most comfortable being present? How would you choose to spend the time with someone?

5. In what ways would you feel comfortable inviting someone into your presence?

6. Describe your level of awareness of Jesus' presence in your life.

7. Write down some things you can do to remind yourself of his presence with you and how his presence makes a difference. (I had a friend who spent several weeks setting an alarm on her wristwatch to go off every hour to remind her to think about God being with her. It effectively reminded her and those with her as well.)

Chapter 14

Extravagance

No eye has seen, no ear has heard, no mind has conceived
what God has prepared for those who love him.

1 CORINTHIANS 2:9

When I first feasted on the visual delights of *The Wizard of Oz*, I was enthralled with the final moments of the movie as Dorothy reaches the Emerald City. Even before the colorized version was created, the images of a dazzlingly beautiful dwelling place leaped off the screen. The streets shimmered, and the palace loomed above the outlying meadows and streams. The benevolent potentate, the Wizard, ruled over all with love and kindness.

As a girl, I carried that image of Oz in my mind's eye as a picture of what heaven might be like: shimmering and glittering and bright. When Jack died, I received a telegram from Billy Graham that included the words, "Heaven must be a little closer." I cried when I first read those words, and each time since. With Jack's death, part of my heart has been touched by heaven. My childhood vision has been transformed from a glittering wonderland into a realm unable to be contained in my thoughts. Words are inadequate to describe what I feel when I think of heaven, except to say that I know it is an extravagantly generous gift from God to us who love him.

There is a saying that warns, "Don't be so heavenly minded you're no earthly good." I think we've become so earthly minded that we're no heavenly good. We have forgotten what a really enormous deal it is that we get to live in heaven forever. We've neglected to think about heaven in ways that stir our spirits toward extravagant giving.

I'm not advocating that we lounge around in gossamer gowns by tranquil pools of spring water as we gaze longingly into heaven. Being heavenly minded means that we include the reality of heaven in our thinking. We embrace the good news that God rewards lavishly.

We don't have to wait till we get to heaven to experience God's extravagant giving; it's available to us right now. As we grow in relationship with God, we receive spiritual abundance that is beyond what we could ever imagine, and we understand that he is an extravagantly generous giver.

When our prayers seem unanswered, we can forget about those times when we were amazed at how fully God answered us, times when he did more than we could ask or think. One such time for me happened in the past two weeks. My daughter Lisa was expecting her second child on July 25. She had told me months before that she was hoping the baby would be born on July 14, her father's birthday—her father and his two brothers were all born on July 14 of different years!

Lisa's birthday is July 13, so she always had a joint celebration with her father until his death. Now she was hoping for this new baby to come on that important day in her life. I listened to her but dismissed her hope as an unlikely event since the July 14 was 11 days before the baby was due.

On July 13 our whole family celebrated Lisa's birthday with dinner at our house. After dinner, Lisa asked us all to join her for a brisk walk so she could help get the baby's arrival going. As we walked, I reminded Lisa that she really couldn't do anything to make the baby be born the next day.

"I know," she smiled, "but I have a lot of people praying for it."

"Yeah, I know," I replied. "I'm praying, too, but I don't think you should count on it."

That night I crawled into bed around 11:00 P.M. At 12:10 A.M., the phone rang.

"Mom, this is Chadd," my son-in-law said in a you-won't-believe-this tone.

"I got into bed at 11:56," he said as I pictured the large digital clock on their dresser. "At exactly midnight, Lisa's water broke! We're getting ready to go to the hospital, and she wants you to meet us there."

I bolted out of bed.

Jackson Alexander Miller, named after his grandfather Jack, was born at 4:01 A.M. on July 14, 1997. That beautiful, healthy, baby boy—and the timing of his arrival—is an extravagantly generous gift from God. God gave Lisa the desire of her heart. There is no other explanation for me. We all would have been thrilled with Alex's arrival on any day, but to have him arrive when he did was abundance at its best.

RELIEVING FEARS ABOUT EXTRAVAGANT GIVING

I suspect that some of you are fidgeting in your chairs at the word *extravagance*. You may feel nervous that I'm endorsing flagrant spending or indulgent lifestyles. Your fears are certainly justified. Some people just don't know when to stop spending money, and others spoil their children with too many material goodies. Some indulge in lavish lifestyles that cost fortunes to maintain.

Maybe, though, you are attaching meaning to the word *extravagance* that God doesn't intend. Maybe there are ways to give extravagant gifts that aren't overdoing or spoiling or indulging.

I once met a woman at a conference who talked to me about a friend of hers and how he spoiled his daughter. I asked her what she meant by "spoiled."

"Every year on her birthday her father sends her a dozen roses."

I waited for more of an explanation, but that was it.

Surprised, I told the woman, "I think that sending roses is a beautiful gesture that his daughter will treasure all her life. Why do you think he's spoiling her by doing that?"

She looked offended that I had not agreed with her, shook her head, and walked off.

We're so quick to judge others. I do it too. My preference would be to give extravagant, lavish gifts all the time—materially and otherwise. Let's have a party, a parade, an extravaganza the likes of which no one has ever seen! I have to temper myself in one direction, and those of you who are fearful about giving in big ways may need to open yourself up in other ways. The key is balance.

WHAT ARE GIFTS OF EXTRAVAGANCE?

Gifts of extravagance aren't given every day. They are the exception, the icing on the cake, the curtain call, the brass ring that comes around once in a while. Extravagances are the touches on others that shower them with an abundance of love and say, *This time I've pulled out all the stops.*

Giving gifts of extravagance fills the giver with the giddy expectation of bestowing unexpected abundance on another, and receiving gifts of extravagance touches the receiver with the wonder of unrestrained love.

Extravagant giving is unexpected. It springs from the overflowing heart that seizes an opportunity to give just for the sake of giving.

Years ago I was sitting at a restaurant counter, eating breakfast with a girlfriend. We were at a convention, and the hotel was bustling with people. No tables were available, so we waited patiently at our counter seats for our hassled waitress to take our orders.

"You look really upset," Jill said to the waitress.

"Oh, I am," the young woman replied. "I rode to work on my bike today, and my brand-new compact fell out of my pocket. It cost eight dollars and it's gone."

At the end of our meal, Jill added eight dollars in cash to our check that came to only about five dollars.

"What are you doing?" I asked.

"I'm giving her money for a new compact. Maybe it will encourage her," Jill smiled.

A tip that was more than the bill itself—extravagant and wonderful! We won't know this side of heaven how that waitress responded, but I suspect she was touched by the stranger who passed her way that day.

Some women are extravagant givers in their attention to noticing small things others might like or appreciate. These are material gifts, but they aren't given for special events—they're just given from hearts that thought of certain people as they went about their day.

My daughter Lara pays attention to things that interest people or that they admire, and she gives them gifts connected to those preferences. I love Paris, so she is frequently picking up things for me that have Paris landmarks on them. She is the aunt-of-the-year to Justin and often spends time with him just for fun and gives him gifts that thrill him; stickers, cards, books. Lara's Aunt Jayne is a dog-lover, so Lara sent a birthday box of goodies to Ben, Aunt Jayne's dog, on his birthday. Jayne was thrilled at this gift that demonstrated Lara's love for her.

Bobbe is another extravagant giver. She says that her love language is gifts, and those around her attest that she often gives them presents for no reason. Bobbe travels a lot and picks up gifts that remind her of different people. Sometimes she buys items that touch her, and she holds on to them to give to just the right person. Giving is a part of her nature and conveys a heart so full of God's love that it spills out to others.

Linda is another extravagant giver. She and her husband, Monte, were having dinner with us when my husband, Steve, started talking about his next book project. He excitedly told about his interest in Celtic spirituality and how intrigued he was with this particular people. A few weeks later Linda gave Steve a voluminous, historical novel about the Celts which she had reread and underlined for him. She had made margin notes and comments throughout the book that described intricate details about Celtic life and belief. Linda, unsolicited, had given an extravagant amount of time and attention to detail to help Steve.

When asked about women of a generous spirit, Sarah spoke of her friend Joy. "She knew that I love Monet paintings, and I didn't have many pictures in our house. She went out and found a copy of a Monet for seven dollars. She bought it, dusted it, and made it look great for me. She made my week."

None of these gifts were items the recipients needed. They were extras—loving touches that made a difference in their lives.

We are not all inclined, nor can we all afford, to be material gift givers. But those who give extravagantly in this way touch others with the fullness in their hearts. They are low-key and genuine in their desire to give for the sheer joy of giving and for the pleasure of those receiving.

A couple I know, Andy and Molly, give to charities at Christmas, but one year they decided to give in a unique way. They wanted to give presents to children in an orphanage who would not usually receive special gifts. They found a home for children who were between foster homes.

In talking with the director, they learned that fifteen children between the ages of seven and twelve lived at the home. Several had been there for a few years because it is difficult to place older children. Andy and Molly told the director they wanted the children to pick out what they wanted for Christmas and asked that she give them the list. They had decided to spend about thirty-five dollars on each child.

They didn't want the children to know where the gifts came from but would include a letter with the gifts that explained what Christmas was and that they were loved.

As Christmas approached, the director called Andy and Molly to tell them that she had trouble getting the children to actually pick out thirty-five dollars worth of presents.

"These children are not used to having this much spent on them," she explained. "They usually receive little packages of gum and candy, and that's it."

Andy and Molly got all the presents requested and delivered them to the director. They never met the children because they wanted to stay anonymous, but the director called them several days after Christmas. "Your generosity has changed the lives of some of these children," the director began. "One boy has stopped wetting the bed, and another has changed his rebellious behavior. They were all amazed when they opened the gifts and saw that they had received all they had asked for. Some cried, and others said they didn't know anybody loved anybody that much. It was a wonderful thing you did."

The director went on to say that people are often afraid to give big gifts to these children because they think the children will be disappointed when they don't continue to receive what they ask for. But these children were deeply touched by this overwhelming generosity.

If we pay attention, any of us can learn to be extravagant givers. We can listen to people dream or admire something or make I-wish statements. Some of these wishes will be material; others will be wishes that life could have a touch of serendipity now and again.

TURNING THE ORDINARY INTO THE EXTRAORDINARY

Extravagance can turn the ordinary into the extraordinary. Everyday events are transformed into festive occasions when generous women shower their loving touches on our lives.

My friend Susan is a woman with amazing gifts of extravagance, and she gives these gifts while spending little money. Her love of life and creativity inspire her to flavor her relationships with unique touches that communicate how she values individuals and enjoys making them feel special.

Susan expresses her gifts as an interior designer, but her friends also are beneficiaries of her extravagant giving in many other ways.

One year Susan surprised her friend Traci on her birthday by transporting a party from her house to a gazebo in a park. Susan arranged for everyone to meet at the park where she had already decorated the gazebo with gauzy material, bows, lace, and flowers. She had packed a basket with china, crystal, and linen tablecloths and napkins. Susan already had these items so she didn't spend much money at all on this elaborate party.

What she did spend was her time in creating a setting that she knew Traci would love. A party at her house would have been a lovely and thoughtful gift, but the decorated gazebo was an extravagance that spoke special love to Traci.

Susan and I have traveled together, and I am always surprised at what she pulls out of her suitcase. She insists on making the drabbest hotel rooms shimmer with warmth. She brings framed photographs, candles, and buys fresh flowers whenever she can.

Even meeting Susan for coffee can become an event. She encourages meetings at cafés with ambiance—her favorite word and the name for her decorating business—instead of just grabbing a cup of coffee at a restaurant. She allows time to engage in meaningful conversation and express her interest in your life. She vulnerably shares her heart, crying and laughing and giving her full attention to the person she is with.

Her very manner is extravagant: She arrives on time and enthusiastically greets you, she never looks at her watch, she is engaged and attentive, and she leaves with promises of meeting again soon. An ordinary meeting for coffee is graciously transformed by her extravagance.

Annie is another woman who loves to turn the ordinary into the extraordinary. She sees a silver lining in every dark cloud. "The kids and I missed our flight connection in St. Louis a few weeks ago," she began, "but we had a ball anyway. We didn't have our luggage and were dead tired from our trip back East. People at the airport were really grumbling and carrying on, which I don't get. I mean, what can you do?

"We picked up our little complimentary cosmetic packets from the airline and went to our designated hotel. The hotel restaurant was closed, and we were starved. So I got a lot of change and raided the vending machine. We took all our junk food back to the room and had a picnic on the floor. It wasn't the most healthy meal, but we turned a bad night into a fun one."

Annie has an extravagant attitude about making the best of any situation. She was exhausted and had good reason to be irritable with the unexpected overnight stay in St. Louis. Instead, she turned her attitude from negative to positive and brought life to a difficult situation.

Life will go on without these extra-special touches. But women of a generous spirit know that extravagance communicates great value to the recipients. We experience their responses when they are pampered, given more than they need, or abundantly loved.

God loves us extravagantly. As we grow to realize and enjoy his love, may we be filled with a desire to give extravagantly to others.

Questions and Suggestions

1. Write down your feelings when you read the word *extravagant*.

2. When have you been the recipient of extravagant giving?

3. When have you given in extravagant ways?

4. Think about some extravagance you can give some unsuspecting person. Do it.

Chapter 15

Loving Truthfulness

As iron sharpens iron,
so one man sharpens another.

PROVERBS 27:17

When we live in truthfulness, our thoughts and actions are consistent with our beliefs. When we give loving truthfulness, we encourage others to live with congruity, to align their thoughts and actions with their beliefs.

Women of a generous spirit understand that truth sometimes causes pain. No one enjoys being corrected or relishes confrontation with a friend who has observed an inconsistency. But women of a generous spirit know that life-giving love is honest and touches others in ways that change them for the better.

"YOU'RE IGNORING WHAT YOU KNOW IS TRUE"

Diane had been Kelly's mentor for years. Diane was several years older and had experienced some of the heartache Kelly was going through. Both women had been divorced when their husbands left them for other women. Diane had happily remarried after five years of dating. Kelly was newly divorced and just beginning to date.

Diane watched and listened as Kelly met and dated several men. She showed no particular interest until Allan came along. Allan had never been married, was handsome and engaging, and worked with a Christian ministry. All the single women that Kelly knew considered Allan a prime catch.

Kelly was thrilled when Allan asked her out and excitedly told Diane that she thought this guy could be the *one*. Diane cautioned her to slow down her emotions, but Kelly was well on her way to choreographing the perfect romance.

"Oh, Diane, he's fabulous," Kelly gushed the morning after her first date with Allan. She spent the next half-hour describing Allan as a white knight in shining armor who swept into her life at just the right time. "I've been so down, and he makes me feel so good."

Red flags popped up all over Diane's brain, but she could tell her friend was too emotionally embroiled with romantic fantasies to pay any attention.

Kelly and Allan dated for over a year before their relationship ended. During that time, Diane watched Kelly make one poor decision after another. Allan was indeed charming and desirable. Kelly was indeed smitten. But he wanted nothing to do with commitment, and Kelly wanted to remarry.

Diane spent many hours in heart-wrenching conversation with

Kelly, attempting to reveal to her that her relationship with Allan was unhealthy. Kelly admitted that she and Allan were walking on a narrow ledge with their sexual activity. As the months rolled by and Allan refused to talk about marriage, Kelly became more and more distressed.

Finally Diane lovingly confronted her with the truth of her situation.

"You are ignoring what you know is true," she began. "You and Allan are not living in ways consistent with both of your beliefs. You're excusing your actions because you are hoping to marry him. And you're making decisions based on your emotions instead of on what you know is right."

Kelly received Diane's words and agreed that she and Allan needed to change their relationship. They limited their sexual activity but still saw each other. Kelly continued to hope against hope that he would soon want to marry. She was still in agony.

"I will continue to be your friend and walk with you through the pain of this relationship," Diane told her, "but you need to realize that your pain is your own doing."

Diane's words stung Kelly, and tears slid down her face as she nodded an acknowledgment. Diane went on to lovingly point out to Kelly all the inconsistencies in her relationship with Allan. He spent a great deal of time with Kelly but wasn't willing to make a commitment; he said he cared for her but was emotionally unavailable; he said he didn't really want to date other women but flirted all the time.

"Knowing all this, Kelly, if you continue to see him, you are choosing to stay in this pain," Diane concluded.

Kelly received Diane's loving truthfulness and ended her relationship with Allan. She was in pain for several months after they separated. Kelly began to hear about women whom Allan had dated quietly while he was still seeing her. She recognized that her emotions had deceived her into believing a lie. Allan had never intended to marry her, and he had never led her to believe that he would.

Her friend's words had revealed the truth to her—and that painful truth became a gift of integrity. Kelly grieved over her duplicitous behavior and asked God's forgiveness. She looked back at how she had slipped into the relationship with Allan and determined not to be so easily deluded again. She asked Diane to hold her accountable and help her keep her promises to live in ways consistent with her commitment to Christ.

A woman of a generous spirit, Diane risked rejection from her friend in order to draw Kelly to goodness.

Sometimes our desire to confront others with the truth overshadows our obligation to check our own attitude about speaking out.

SEASON WITH LOVE AND HUMILITY

It feels good to be right. A selfish arrogance can seep into our hearts, and we delight when some truth we have predicted comes to pass. We may not utter the words, but we are thinking, *I told you!*

Such a response is the opposite of what God is calling us toward. Women of a generous spirit are humble. They know that we are all guilty before God. Diane didn't try to nail Kelly with the truth of her mistakes. She came to her with a loving spirit that was concerned for Kelly's well-being; she did not have a critical, self-righteous spirit.

In Ephesians 4, Paul talks about attaining the "whole measure of the fullness of Christ" (v. 13). When we have that fullness, we will no longer be tossed about by deceptive teaching but, "Instead, speaking the truth in love, we will in all things grow up into him who is the Head, that is, Christ" (v. 15).

Givers of loving truthfulness don't yell or point fingers at those they are confronting. They don't shame or embarrass. Instead, they meet privately and speak gently. They know that the way they speak the truth matters. They have evaluated their motives to be sure they are not speaking out of pride. They know that if they flavor the truth with love and humility, the receiver may be touched with love that impacts and empowers her.

WALKING WITH OTHERS

Diane committed to walk with Kelly while she was going through the tough time of breaking up with Allan. She spent many hours listening to Kelly cry and labor through the pain of a disappointing relationship. Diane kept Kelly's struggle confidential. She provided a safe place for Kelly to fully express her pain and know it would not end up as a request on a prayer chain.

Diane was also vulnerable with Kelly about some of her own past struggles. She identified with Kelly's desire to remarry and with the challenge of adult dating. It took a long time for Kelly to heal from the pain of her broken relationship with Allan, but Diane's commitment to her helped her experience healing.

We are often tempted to walk away from people who are making poor choices. It's easier to turn our heads and dismiss them than to bring up touchy issues. But generous-spirited women get their hands dirty in the fray. They struggle with friends who are struggling within themselves. They travel over the same conversational ground again and again as a friend tries to unravel tangled emotions. They keep loving, even when someone disagrees with their observations.

I recently risked telling a friend that I was troubled by a relationship in her life. She disagrees with me but is willing to talk about it. The situation is clouded because it is lived out in her emotions, not her actions. But she talks in ways that reveal her feelings.

We have reached different conclusions about what her feelings reveal. Because of the level of friendship and the love we have for each other, we are able to walk together in that friendship and continue to talk. We are staying in the fray together. The truth of the situation hasn't become clear yet, but when it does, it will bloom in a garden of love.

Because I love her, I was willing to risk rejection from her in order to save her from making a choice that she would regret later. Sometimes this is easier to do than at other times.

RISKING REJECTION

"I wish I had said something," Greta said. "I watched a good friend lose her job because she was being really negligent. She missed a lot of days and was irresponsible about her work. I said nothing because I didn't want to hurt her feelings. Now I wish I had."

We have no way of knowing how Greta's friend would have responded had she been confronted. But Greta wishes she had risked speaking up because it might have helped her friend. They might have been able to talk about it and solve some of her friend's work issues.

"If she had gotten mad at me, I would have been unhappy," Greta said, "but at least I would know that I had tried to help her. This way I just feel guilty for not talking to her."

We risk rejection when we speak a painful truth, but the risk is one that generous women are willing to take. Sometimes they are rewarded with a deeper relationship like the one Diane and Kelly experienced. Other times they continue to work through tough issues with friends who disagree. And in some instances, the friendships end.

"Danielle's children were out of control," Nan said. "They were rude and obnoxious all the time. I finally said something to her. She just blew up. She said that my evaluation wasn't true, and I was just too strict a parent. It ended our friendship."

Some areas of life are more delicate than others. Parenting is perhaps on the top of that fragile list. The riskier the topic, the more we need divine guidance to know when to speak and when to keep quiet.

THE NEED FOR SUPERNATURAL DISCERNMENT

I believe that there is absolute truth. For instance, I believe that God is love and that he wants us to love each other. I also believe that there are various applications of truth that God allows. It is an absolute truth that we are to love each other, but there are many ways we can express that love. The most loving thing I might do for one person is to confront her with a truth, and the most loving thing I might do for another friend is to keep quiet.

So if I were to say to you, "You should always confront a friend with loving truthfulness," I would be oversimplifying a potentially complicated situation.

Because they recognize the complexity of their relationships, women of a generous spirit bring their concerns for others to God. They don't react quickly or rely on their own intuition. We all know that we can be wrong. Sometimes we are even sure we are hearing from God, only later to find out we were wrong.

Supernatural discernment is available to us in our relationship with God. Paul's prayer for the Philippian church is one I have prayed for my children since they were born: "And this is my prayer: that your love may abound more and more in knowledge and depth of insight, so that you may be able to discern what is best and may be pure and blameless until the day of Christ, filled with the fruit of righteousness that comes through Jesus Christ—to the glory and praise of God" (Philippians 1:9-11).

Knowledge and depth of insight lead to discernment. We receive both through our relationship with God. Paul isn't talking about worldly knowledge or insight found in books. He's talking about spiritual understanding that God reveals to those who love and know him.

When women of a generous spirit bring their concerns about friends before God, they do so with open hearts, without a preconceived agenda. They admit their own fallibility. They talk with him, pray, read, wait, write down their thoughts—they repeat the seven steps in chapter 6.

The result? Sometimes they speak in loving truthfulness, and sometimes they keep quiet. Usually the depth of relationship with the other person is a big factor in the decision to speak up or not. People do many things that are inconsistent with the truth of God, but it's none of my business. I can silently pray for them, but I have no basis of relationship to go to them.

One woman told me she prays that a friend she is concerned about will come to her and ask her advice. "That way I am able to be honest without being intrusive. It doesn't always happen, but often I pray they will ask—and they ask."

Loving truthfulness is about longing for others to enjoy God's very best for them. It isn't about being right or straightening out the world. It's about loving people enough to draw them to God's love and to experience that love in the integrity of relationship with others and with him.

Questions and Suggestions

1. Write down any areas in your own life where you feel you lack integrity.

2. Determine to make changes so that your life and your beliefs are congruent. Ask a woman friend for help.

3. Write down the names of people you know for whom you have concerns about their integrity. Commit to pray for them daily.

4. Repeat the seven steps in chapter 6, seeking supernatural discernment about whether to talk with any of these people or not.

5. Pray for a spirit of love and not criticism.

Chapter 16

Provision

Riches do not consist in the possession of treasures,
but in the use of them.

Napolean Bonaparte

"My mom notices the needs of others. She consciously looks for ways to provide things that are needed. For example, she might hear that someone's car needs to be fixed, so she calls them and asks if they need a ride."

Cindy and I had been discussing what it means to be a woman of a generous spirit, and our conversation had turned to helping meet the needs of others. Cindy began to tell me about her mother, who is a role model for her about how to be a life-giver. "Mom also has a tablecloth ministry. When she goes to a fabric store she buys yards of material on sale. Then she makes beautiful tablecloths and napkins to match and donates them to her church. No one would ever ask her to do that, but they wouldn't go out and buy them either."

Cindy has inherited her mother's ability to see the needs of others, and I was the recipient of her generosity when she and her family stayed with us for a week a few summers ago. At the end of the week, Cindy stripped the beds, washed the sheets, and remade the beds. She washed all the towels they had used and cleaned the bathrooms. I wasn't aware of what she was doing. When she and her family left, I discovered what she'd done because there was no cleaning left for me to do. Her provision was a generous gift to me at a very busy time.

Marilyn is another generous spirit who sees a need and tries to meet it in ways that best serve the person she wants to help. "I have a friend with two small children and another one on the way. Recently her husband was in the hospital, and I offered to take the kids, but she was flustered about them being at my house. So I brought them to the hospital and watched them there. I think you need to serve in the way the person needs to be served, not in the way you think they need to be served."

Generous women care about others, including people in the greater community. But since it's impossible to give to everyone who has a need, they must wrestle with how to prioritize their giving.

WHAT TO GIVE TO WHOM

Because we can't do everything, we constantly face the challenge of deciding what we must say no to. Requests for financial resources pour in, and our phones ring, frequently heralding another call from a church committee that needs help. On Sundays we hear of more needs as well as entreaties to fill vacant positions of responsibility. Then we read a book like this that suggests reading the newspaper and reaching out to the needy in our communities! It's exhausting just to think about all we could be doing.

Your priorities are unique to you, and mine are unique to me. Each of us must decide for ourselves how we spend our time, energy, and financial resources. I used to automatically plunge into anything I was asked to do. There was a time when I had commitments at church every single day of the week. All the needs were legitimate, all provided helpful services, all interested me—yet I couldn't give my best to any because I was so exhausted.

I needed to learn to winnow such requests and to choose according to what I believe God wants me to do. I've found that when I do, I can say no without feeling guilty over the decision.

Paul commands us: "Each [woman] should give what [she] has decided in [her] heart to give, not reluctantly or under compulsion, for God loves a cheerful giver" (2 Corinthians 9:7). When I read this verse, I usually focus on the word *cheerful,* and I've overlooked the word *compulsion,* yet it may be more important. Many times I've given because I just felt like I *had* to. Instead of thinking, going to God for his insight, and waiting, I compulsively responded to needs because they existed and I thought I could fill them.

This verse also says we are to give as we have decided in our hearts. It would be easy to misinterpret this to mean we are to give in all the areas that touch us emotionally. But remember, godly giving flows from our heart connection with God, not just our emotional response. "And God is able to make all grace abound to you, so that in all things at all times, having all that you need, you will abound in every good work" (2 Corinthians 9:8).

By God's grace we are able to be the generous women he wants us to be. We receive his grace as we relate to him through prayer, Bible reading, and meditation. His grace touches our hearts and informs our minds about the choices we must make in providing for needs.

When I'm interacting with God about where to give my time or resources, I often use the following adaptation of the steps in chapter 6:

1. Meet with him: Go to a quiet place to specifically meet with God about how to choose what to give to whom.
2. Ask yourself questions about how you feel about the various opportunities to give.
3. Write down how you feel.
4. Reflect: Sit quietly with Jesus and just wait.
5. Write down your thoughts or impressions.
6. Take one step of obedience: Don't respond emotionally or out of a sense of guilt or fear of what others will say. Obediently do what you believe *God* wants you to do.

Through our wrestling with God, the answers come. Without God's help in the process, we will continue to make choices out of compulsion or emotional pulls. Cheerful giving results from giving from a full heart and in ways that are consistent with God's individual guidance.

AVOIDING THE MONEY TRAP

Obviously, money provides the means to meet many needs. It is also a common way in which we are asked to help, and if you are like me, it's easy to be overwhelmed by the numerous requests for financial support. God tells us to give as we have decided in our hearts, yet sometimes we give as if we were playing Russian roulette. Rather than involving God in the process, we put all the requests on the table and spin a wheel.

Sometimes we are asked to loan money to friends or family. The danger is that the friendship or family relationship may be put in jeopardy. They intend to pay us back, but what if they don't? Unexpected calamities happen, more needs arise, and some people are just not responsible about their financial affairs.

In the Sermon on the Mount, Jesus has something to say about lending money. He is talking about lending to strangers, but his words are worth considering when we are asked to loan money to friends and family: "And if you lend to those from whom you expect repayment, what credit is that to you? Even 'sinners' lend to 'sinners,' expecting to be repaid in full. But love your enemies, do good to them, and lend to them without expecting to get anything back" (Luke 6:34-35).

If we borrow money from someone, we are responsible to repay it. But as generous women, what are we to do if the people to whom we loan money come to us and confess that they can't repay us? We give, from the very beginning, with no expectation of repayment. We don't have to tell people that we are thinking this way, but if we give without expectations of repayment, then we protect the relationship. We free others to deal with God about their responsibilities. We give with the unspoken attitude that the loan is actually a gift.

A young woman asked me recently if I thought she and her husband should loan money to her parents. I asked her what she and her husband would do if the money wasn't repaid.

"I don't know, but I think we'd be upset," she replied.

"Would that damage your relationship with your parents?" I asked her.

"Oh yeah, it would. They'd be embarrassed."

"Then I think you need to decide either to loan them the money, but be willing to view it as a gift, or don't loan them the money."

She and her husband talked about it, prayed about it, and decided to loan her parents the money. They agreed that the relationship was more important than the repayment and silently considered the loan a gift.

"They did pay us back," she later told me with a smile. "But the great thing was that we had no stress about it. We gave them the money and never mentioned the repayment again. They sent it on their own, which was great, but I think we would have been okay even if they hadn't."

Often relationships are key in determining how we give of our finances. The closer we are, the more heartfelt engagement we experience. We will be giving not only to strangers but to people we care about. Friends and family will hold a higher priority.

Organizations also solicit our help. Our hearts will be more drawn to organizations that provide help in areas that touch us. As before, we bring the requests to God, meet with him, and involve him in the decision. Our money is a vehicle to help others, but the generosity comes from full hearts.

WHAT ABOUT THE POOR?

Jesus said, "I tell you the truth, whatever you did for one of the least of these brothers of mine, you did for me" (Matthew 25:40).

Several years ago Steve and I met Darryl, a homeless man who had done some yard work for a couple from our church. We decided to help him out by employing him to do similar work for us.

Darryl lived in a broken-down van that was parked behind a bar near downtown Colorado Springs. The owner of the bar let Darryl use the phone occasionally so he could connect with the people trying to help him. Steve called the bar and arranged to pick up Darryl and bring him to our house.

For about three months Steve would go to get Darryl and take him back to the van after he worked in our yard. During that time I struggled with my discomfort when Darryl was around. I didn't have a lot of contact with him, but he did join us for meals, and he sometimes showered in the house before leaving. Steve was the main connection and understood my uneasiness about having this stranger around.

After the first month, Darryl started to ask Steve for additional money. We tried to take him to the grocery store and buy things he needed instead of giving him cash. Darryl openly admitted that he had a drinking problem and spent most of his money on alcohol. Then Darryl called several times after midnight and asked Steve to come pick him up or bail him out of jail.

Darryl finally got in some kind of trouble and left town. I was relieved and, at the same time, felt guilty that I had so little compassion for this poor man. I know that he is not necessarily representative of all homeless people, but he is the only homeless person I have ever known. Perhaps ignorance is a major factor in my discomfort.

Giving to the poor and disenfranchised is often messy, uncomfortable business that exposes us to a sometimes seedy side of life we would prefer to ignore. I readily admit my own conflict with God's admonition to take care of those less fortunate than I am. The politics involved with this issue further confuse me. I hear about human need and feel one way. Then I hear a political argument that presents a different view, and I feel another way. Some say people who don't have food need food, and I want to give them food; others say people who don't have food will abuse the system and you if you help them, and I become fearful.

I am in the middle of sorting out how God wants me to participate in providing for the poor. I don't know the answer yet, but I do know that a battle rages. Politics, religion, and human need bubble together in a pot of conflict: welfare, welfare reform, medical aid for indigents, help for unwed mothers.

As women who desire to be life-givers, we need to engage with God in *all* aspects of our giving. Whether the need is large or small, financial or otherwise, we need God's help in how to respond. Rather than ignoring needs because we feel overwhelmed or confused, let's come into God's presence and ask him to touch our hearts so that we can touch others in all parts of our culture.

Questions and Suggestions

1. How do you now decide what to give to whom?

2. Determine to meet with God and put requests before him.

3. If you haven't already, begin to evaluate how you (and your family) handle issues of financial giving.

4. Write a paragraph describing your feelings about the disenfranchised of our society.

5. Pray and ask God what he would have you do personally.

Chapter 17

Legacy

> *But as for you, the Lord took you and brought you*
> *out of the iron-smelting furnace, out of Egypt,*
> *to be the people of his inheritance, as you now are.*
>
> DEUTERONOMY 4:20

As John Donne observed, "No man is an island." We have been impacted by those who lived on this earth before us, and we impact those who will live longer than we will. You and I are part of a bigger picture. The women we are now matter for more than just the season of our earthly lives. We will touch generations to come, as we have been touched.

Such are the gifts of legacy, gifts offered through our words, attitudes, values, behavior, and wisdom. They give our lives continuity. They transcend death and carry our influence into the future.

WORDS OF LEGACY

Words my grandmother spoke to me over fifty years ago still ring in my ears. She died when I was ten years old, but I remember her well.

Nanny lived with us, and I spent a lot of time with her. She was a gentle woman who never complained. She often told me:

"Be kind to other people."

"I love you."

"Listen to your mother."

"Remember to say your prayers."

Last year I heard a television interview with Maya Angelou in which she talked about the power of words. In her wonderful, rolling voice she spoke of the walls holding words and how she doesn't allow unkind talk in her house. She went on to explain that when a word is spoken, it is out. It is done. Good or evil has been released.

My grandmother spoke words of goodness, words that gave me life. I cherish them.

But not everyone spoke such words to me. I remember other words as well, words of hurt spoken decades ago that have left an imprint on my soul.

Because they understand the lasting power of words, women of a generous spirit choose their words wisely. They think before they speak. They resist repeating bad reports or passing on gossip. They know the power of the tongue to heal or destroy: "With the tongue we praise our Lord and Father, and with it we curse men, who have been made in God's likeness. Out of the same mouth come praise and cursing. My brothers, this should not be" (James 3:9-10).

As we become women of a generous spirit, we will hear ourselves with more clarity. So often we speak idly, as if our words don't matter. But as we grow in deeper relationship with God, we will begin to grasp the power our words have. They will be repeated after we are gone. What will our words say about us?

ATTITUDES OF LEGACY

Sometimes words, in and of themselves, don't convey ill. Sometimes it's the way the words are said, the attitude conveyed.

Our children, grandchildren, and those around us can absorb our attitudes and incorporate fragments of them into their own lives.

Women of a generous spirit cultivate attitudes that give life. They are forgiving, gracious, kind, loving, giving, compassionate, and humble.

"My mother was a really generous woman," Jean said. "She was always cooking meals for neighbors and offering to watch their kids for them. She volunteered at church and just gave a lot. But the thing I remember is that she never talked about it. If someone asked her what she did, she downplayed her giving. She was humble.

"I don't know if I inherited her attitude, but I am sure aware of it. I want to be humble and not brag about what I do. I admire how she was, and I want to hang on to that attitude myself."

Our attitudes are conveyed by a myriad of expressions. People notice our facial expressions, our body language, our manner of speaking, our silence, our actions. We have all experienced being in a room and seeing someone walk in with an "attitude." The person doesn't have to open her mouth to convey to the whole room how she feels.

Our attitude impacts those close to us. They receive the messages our attitudes send and carry them for years.

LEGACY OF OUR VALUES

"My nana doesn't say that," Justin responded to someone on television saying "Shut up."

He's right. I grew up in a home where harsh words were common. I was often told "Shut up" and "You're so stupid." Those unkind words are on my things-we-don't-say list.

Justin's parents don't allow him to say those either, and when he heard those words on television, he also identified that value with me. He's only three years old and already knows well what some of my values are.

One of the challenges in passing on values is to clearly define what we hold dear. If we want to become women of a generous spirit, our values will spring from our relationship with God. Our whole lives will reflect those values.

That is true for everyone. Whenever we read or hear about people, we're given clues about their values. Their actions reveal what is important to them. This morning's news told about some Chinese businessmen who allegedly had given money to the

Democratic Party. At the wrap-up of the story, the news commentator said China places great value on friendship, or perceived friendship, with an American president. The alleged actions of those businessmen reflect that value.

We are told that the great English preacher Charles Spurgeon had teams of people praying in the basement of his church around the clock. We can conclude from that practice that Spurgeon valued the practice of prayer.

Sometimes people say they value something, but their actions prove otherwise. When I went through a dry period spiritually and wasn't spending time with God very often, I still said that I valued time with him. In reality, the value of that practice had slipped away from me. I didn't spend the time, so obviously it wasn't of great value. When I reevaluated my need and desire to focus on my relationship with God, I more highly valued that practice. My behavior reflected that value when I spent more time with him.

What do your actions reveal about your values? If you were to die today, what values would your family and friends remember you for?

MATCHING BEHAVIOR WITH WORDS

The legacy of our values will largely be determined by how closely what we say we value matches how we live.

When we were buying airline tickets years ago, a travel agent told me that Lara could probably pass for younger than she was and, therefore, get a cheaper ticket. It was tempting to save the money—and lots of people do it—but I decided I wouldn't try to deceive the airline. I didn't want my children to lie, so I needed to live in a way consistent with that value.

Pat reflects her value of all human life by volunteering at a crisis-pregnancy center, helping young women choose to give birth to their babies.

Marie is concerned about all kinds of people being treated with respect, so she works in the nursing-home industry, focusing on patients being treated with dignity.

Mike and Kim feel a need to reach people in distant countries with the gospel, so they serve as missionaries in a remote village in Peru.

Women of a generous spirit know what they believe and value, and they live in ways that reflect those values. Those values are a gift to the people in their lives.

LEGACY OF WISDOM

Gifts of wisdom are also wonderful legacies we can pass on.

Our American culture doesn't value the wisdom that comes with age the way that many other cultures do, but women of a generous spirit know the benefit of sitting at the feet of a wise woman. Godly women hold a wealth of advice and knowledge in their minds and hearts that will make our way smoother if we learn from them. All we experience is grist for the mill of future generations. What we struggle with today will be the lessons we teach tomorrow.

God places great worth on attaining wisdom: "Wisdom is supreme; therefore get wisdom. Though it cost all you have, get understanding" (Proverbs 4:7). The wisdom the Bible speaks of comes from knowing God. Our relationship with him is the source of any wisdom we can pass along.

PASSING ON OUR HISTORY

The Bible is unlike any other book for a number of reasons, including divine inspiration. It is also a history of God's people that includes stories of their exploits, failures, trials, successes, encounters with God, and encounters with each other. If each of us were to write a book about her own life, we could not claim divine inspiration. Our stories would be from our human perspective and, undoubtedly, be flawed and contain inaccuracies. But the telling of our life stories is a gift of legacy that can touch our loved ones for generations to come.

As you become intentional about being a woman of a generous spirit, consider writing a "Legacy Journal." This journal will be a book of lessons-I-have-learned that you record for your children or another loved one if you don't have children. You can write in it whenever you want, from now until you are no longer able to write.

Of course, you will need to let someone know of its existence so that it can be given to the desired recipients after you are gone.

There are many beautiful, bound blank journals to choose from, but pick one that reflects your own personal taste. You may be able to fill volumes of these books and leave a whole collection for loved ones.

I have no written accounts of my family's stories, only the verbal ones my parents and grandmother told me. Those memories are priceless, and I love to run them back through my mind as I remember my family.

One of my mother's favorite stories was about the day she brought a horse into the house. Chief was her pet horse. She lived on a farm as a young girl, and Chief was one of the workhorses. He was a big black horse who came readily at my mother's whistle and somehow communicated to her that he favored her over her five brothers.

One day my mother was in the kitchen of the farmhouse, and Chief wandered up to the back door. He butted his nose against the screen and whinnied to my mother. She impulsively opened the door and beckoned him to come in. Chief walked through the door and into the kitchen. My mother led him right through the house and out the front door.

Her father saw her lead Chief out the front door and started screaming. He came running over and was shocked that my mother had simply invited Chief for a stroll through the house. My mother didn't understand the big to-do until her father explained how Chief could have broken a leg if he had fallen through the wooden floorboards.

No one was hurt, and my mother wasn't punished.

She used to tell the story with great delight. That story revealed my mother's love of animals and her special relationship with her father. It also reflected her sense of fun that contributed to her generosity as a mother and grandmother.

There are other stories my family told that are gifts to me and my children. You have those stories too. As parts of our Legacy Journals, they become written documentation of the inheritance we are passing on.

Gifts of legacy fill the giver with the reality of immortality and infuse the receiver with the life-giving love of generations of generosity.

Questions and Suggestions

1. What words (phrases, manner of speech) do you think people associate with you?

2. In what ways might you better choose your words or manner of speech?

3. What attitudes do you now hold that you would not like to see repeated in your children or in others you love?

4. What attitudes would you like to cultivate?

5. What values would your actions reveal?

6. In what ways would you like to change your behavior to match your values?

7. Who do you know who speaks with wisdom? If you don't know anyone, pray for God to bring a wise, godly woman into your life.

8. Buy your first Legacy Journal.

9. Start writing!

An Ongoing Lifestyle

*Let us run with perseverance
the race marked out for us.*

HEBREWS 12:1

A few years ago I took advantage of a special offer at a local health club to sign up for six sessions with a personal trainer at a reduced rate. Marie was a wonderfully encouraging young woman who patiently helped me determine a workout routine that I could do when I traveled. She showed me how to use small weights, how to do exercises and stretches to relieve typical aches that accompany airplane travel, explained about target heart rates for burning fat and much more—all the nitty-gritty of healthy exercise designed to become part of my lifestyle.

I followed her advice and reveled in newfound levels of energy, determining never again to become a plane-potato and suffer the stiffening consequences. Then I got busy. I began to let exercise sessions slip from being a priority. Soon I wasn't working out even when I was home. My zeal to make exercise a part of my ongoing lifestyle had weakened to a fleeting thought now and then.

Our best intentions at making lifestyle changes are often thwarted by the return of the familiar. We tend to revert back to what is most natural when life's pace picks up.

Hebrews 12:1 urges us to "run with perseverance." That word perseverance forewarns us that the race we are called to run will be challenging. We would have no need to persevere if that were not true.

One of the most difficult aspects of becoming women of a generous spirit is keeping on keeping on. Giving is costly. It is also contrary to much of society's directives to put ourselves first.

But remember: Becoming a woman of a generous spirit is a process, not a destination. We don't one day become the women God wants us to be and then rest on that accomplishment.

If you want to continue this process of becoming a woman of a generous spirit, remind yourself what it means to touch others with life. Remember, giving ebbs and flows. Sometimes you will need to receive rather than give. Continue to know God better while realizing that you will never know him completely this side of heaven, remembering that his vastness requires an ongoing relationship to grow in his wisdom.

You are now well on your way to becoming women of a generous spirit. If you persevere, you will have the opportunity to grow more and more into the woman God wants you to be. And you will experience the fulfillment that comes from relationship with the living God and touching others with his love.

As long as you and I keep trying, thinking, learning, growing, resting, giving, we will be our individual ideal. And we will be recipients of the promise that giving leads to: "Give, and it will be given to you. A good measure, pressed down, shaken together and running over, will be poured into your lap. For with the measure you use, it will be measured to you" (Luke 6:38).

Each of us can continue to grow and enjoy the richness of life-giving love we receive from God and give to others. Our lifestyles will be forever changed as long as we allow him to fill us up so we can give from that overflow.

Remember: You are the ideal. Right now you have all you need just being you and opening your heart to God and his love. He will fill you and use you. You will touch others. When they hear your name, they will say, She is a woman of a generous spirit!

Chapter 3: When Good Things Go Awry

1. Dr. Henry Cloud and Dr. John Townsend, *Boundaries* (Grand Rapids, Mich.: Zondervan Publishing House, 1992), 95.

2. Ibid., 96.

Chapter 4: Healing Wounds, Relieving Tensions

1. Margaria Fichtner, "The Gospel According to Mailer," Knight-Ridder newspapers, 1 June 1997, sec T & B, 5-6.

2. Leslie Williams, *Night Wrestling* (Dallas: Word Publishing, 1997), 23.

3. Amy Carmichael, *If* (Fort Washington, Penn.: Christian Literature Crusade, 1984), 39.

Chapter 6: How Can I Give and Not Feel Drained?

1. Richard J. Foster, *Celebration of Discipline* (New York: Harper and Row, 1978), 8.

Chapter 7: Be Yourself

1. Elisabeth Elliott, *The Savage My Kinsman* (Ann Arbor, Mich.: Servant Books, 1961), 19.

Chapter 8: Helping Others Encounter God

1. Angela Dire, "Amendment Two Is Heating Up" *Gazette Telegraph*, 1 October 1995, Sec A, 1, 6-7.

2. Michael Hamilton, "The Dissatisfaction of Francis Schaeffer," *Christianity Today*, 3 March 1997, 24.

Chapter 11: Grace

1. Jerry Bridges, *Transforming Grace* (Colorado Springs, Colo.: NavPress, 1991), 44.

2. Ibid., 196.

Chapter 12: Hope

1. David Viscott, M.D., *Emotional Resilience* (New York: Harmony Books, 1996), 63.

2. Joan Winmill Brown, ed., *Dietrich Bonhoeffer: The Martyred Christian* (New York: Collier Books, 1985), 212.

Lois Mowday Rabey is the author of five books and a frequent semi-nar and conference speaker. She speaks on a wide range of topics including: women and midlife issues, emotional and sexual en-tanglements, developing healthy self-esteem, hope in time of crisis, widowhood, living and learning through loss, single parenting, and dating as an adult.

Lois also presents a seminar based on this book, *Women of a Generous Spirit.*

For more information, contact:

Lois Rabey

Fax: 719-488-2479

Please include your phone number with your fax, and she will return your call.